# The Game in Wall Street

## and how to play it successfully

"Hoyle" and Clem Chambers

ADVFN BOOKS

# CONTENTS

# PREFACE
# BY CLEM CHAMBERS

This book was written over a hundred years ago.

At a time when the car had just been invented, mass production wasn't discovered, if you needed your appendix removed you would likely die from the operation and there were a mere 1.5 billion people on earth. Money was gold and silver.

Yet for the investor this book is still as true today as it was then.

Mark Twain, a contemporary of this book said, "history doesn't repeat itself, but it does rhyme." He may well have been wrong because many of the lessons in this book are still crucial.

The opening passage is extremely important. When you enter the game of trading or investing you are playing a game against full time skilled professionals. How would you fair in a winner-takes-all game of tennis with Federer? Would you even dare come onto the court?

Of course, many people do not trade or invest because that's exactly what they fear. As you are reading this book you aren't one of them. By reading this book you put yourself in a small minority of participants that actually want to learn the game. As such you have a chance to win as the market then and now remains a place where the-one eyed man is king amongst the blind gamblers.

The stock market is overrun with degenerate gamblers and this is the advantage of the investor or highly skilled trader. It's easier to make money because of it, so that if you play the game correctly you are not prey to the big skilled predators that stalk the field.

How do the predators operate? There are a host of swindles in the market and most of them remain. Some, like insider trading, have become illegal, but like most crimes they are reimagined and rebooted. In 1890 insider trading was legal, but once made illegal it morphed. No alongside illegal insider trading there are "expert networks" and other such constructs that skirt the law.

*The Game on Wall Street* concerns itself with "pool" stocks. You can consider them market manipulated shares. They are identified as stocks that turn over huge volumes for no apparent reason, or rather for no benefit to the companies' business. A $36m market cap company turns over $2 billion in equity in a year.

What is the story?

The narrative is, if you want to gamble, the stock market is a very convenient place to do it. It sounds like business rather than gaming for a start. A stock investor can hold his head up in society, whereas a card player must keep his addiction private. The US has long been a country where gambling is difficult, so the stock market is and always will be the biggest casino around.

This is why these stocks trade so furiously. They are the horses running in a race, and the race being for gamblers, is run by the house.

The obvious thing to do is not play that game.

The game is still on as I write. It has changed little. In the dotcom boom it was imaginary tech business. After the dotcom crash it was imaginary mining companies. In 2013 it's back to the internet again. None of it is illegal today. In 100 years it probably won't be legal but the market will have shifted to another stock equivalent of betting on a raindrop falling down a window pane. However, the stock market is "not a game of chance." The house needs to win but there is no built in house edge. The house edge is manufactured by manipulation.

Manipulation and conspiracy is the watchword of the crazy brigade in any field of endeavor. People are sore losers. People seldom believe they lose because of their own decisions, they feel robbed even when there is no one to blame. As such, believing in manipulation and conspiracy is not necessarily healthy. But it does exist.

In 1893 it was only a handful of companies that were manipulated and so it is today. They stand out like a beacon. Their existence is to draw trade moths to their flame. As such it's easy to steer clear. If you see investors drawn to a stock like the Eloi drawn to the siren in HG Wells' book *The Time Machine*, you know not to follow them. There are plenty of real opportunities to follow, without marching into the den of the Morlocks.

However, this book isn't about avoiding manipulation, it's about understanding it and how it has to follow a set pattern. Once you understand the pattern you can jump on it and ride with the manipulators on its magic carpet.

You can do this.

Funnily enough it's a form of illegal activity that is totally legal. The illegal version is called front running, where a broker buys before your big order so that the price rise caused by you creates for him a small profit.

In this case knowing what manipulators have to do to make their crooked profits, you front-run their plan and profit. This is totally legal as you do not know them or their plan, you just understand the shape of what happens next.

You can do this. In its basic form it is trend following.

Be warned that dicing with a manipulation is a highly skilled game. For a start some manipulations simply do not work. But the idea is sound. Not all manipulations are illegal or rather not all manipulations can be proven as such.

Take a stock on the edge of a major index. A fund can buy that stock consistently driving its price high enough to enter that index. They can then unload to the tracker funds that must own it. Likewise a shorter might push down the price of a weak stock so it falls out of an index. Then buy it back as trackers who must now sell unload. This is why stocks that fall from an index often rally. They rally because the shorts have done their manipulation and must cover. This is not 1893, this is 2013.

By definition the plan laid out in this book to coattail these manipulations looks very much like contrarian investing. That is because the small group of manipulators is the ultimate winner and the large group of traders is the loser. As such you need to run against the herd mentality and run with the manipulators' plan.

Remember, if you win doing this you hurt the manipulator as they make less money.

Yet let's stop here and think again.

This cycle of manipulation is about accumulation and distribution. A large holding is built up, the price is made to rise, the holding is sold at a high price.

This is the cycle today. A fund builds up a big holding, it pays IR and PR people to get press for the stock, their chief spokesman will go on TV and say how smart he and his positions are, the stock rises, they sell out. There is nothing illegal there. However this cycle can be very illegal.

Someone gets a block of cheap stock of a near defunct company, spreads lies and false rumors about the stock, flaunts stock market rules on disclosure, artificially inflates the share price using illegal market manipulation techniques like wash trades, sells out at a profit.

It's the same idea, the same form, the same structure. One is legal, one is illegal. Yet it is the same game and the same outcome. The uninitiated trader ends up buying expensive stock at the top of the market.

# INTRODUCTION.

IN putting forth this little pamphlet the Author has no scheme to work.

He has tried to give, in plain language, the facts, or some of them at least, about the game in Wall Street.

He has made no effort at style in writing. Simple English and the "calling a spade a spade" is what he has striven for.

He does not set up to be a reformer. He accepts human nature as he finds it. He hopes that this little work may save a "lamb" or two from the sacrifice.

He realizes fully that if the public is to be saved at all it cannot be done by declaiming against the business itself, for that has been tried "lo! these many years," to no effect, by the moralists. In fact the present year of grace 1898, after all that has been said, shows a stronger speculative tendency in the public mind than has been seen at any time since our Civil War.

Possibly, if the public learn something about the game, they may avoid making fatal mistakes. If the public should learn to play the game so as to win, that in itself would do more to break it up than anything else could. If "the lambs" *should* carry away a hundred million dollars a year from Wall Street instead of losing that amount there annually as they do now, the managers of the game would have to put up the shutters within two years.

In the hopes that some of the lambs may get a hint or two that will help them, this work is launched with the best wishes of

THE AUTHOR

# THE GAME IN WALL STREET.

# PART I.

IF you, my dear sir, were to join a first-class Whist Club you would be expected to know something about the game would you not? Some of the elementary principles of the play you should understand at least, otherwise you have no business to be in the game with experienced players.

What is true of the game of Whist is not less true of the game in Wall Street. In this latter game the amateur who goes into it without study or knowledge, whether he guesses as to the course prices will take, or whether he be influenced by the "tips" and "points" and "gossip" put forth in financial papers and brokers' letters, is almost sure to lose in the end.

"But," I hear you say, "speculation in Wall Street is not a game of chance or skill as in cards. The ups and downs in the prices of stocks depend on economic laws, on crops, on wars and rumors of wars, on high and low money rates, on a thousand and one factors that no man can absolutely foresee." You say, perhaps, that "the price of stocks is regulated by the laws of supply and demand, just as is the price of cloth or flour or any other commodity. That the trading in stocks is as legitimate and honorable as trading in anything else. In any branch of commerce one tries to buy when prices are low, and sell when they are high, and this is just what one does in stock trading."

We reply to your argument that there is a little truth and much sophistry in it. The factors that you mention as determining the prices of stocks have an undoubted influence, but, as you will see before you finish these pages, these commercial factors are not the determining influences directing the course of the stock market.

The people who run the game allow for these factors and arrange their plans in accordance with them, but the general course of prices on the Stock Exchange is determined by human intelligence and not by chance or natural conditions.

Let us consider for a moment the argument put forward by the apologist for trading in stocks, by which he seeks to show that the business is a legitimate one, and one which is governed by the same economic laws as is commercial trading in general.

There is, to be sure, a legitimate trading in stocks. If A buys one hundred shares in N. Y. C., or W. U., or St. Paul as an investment, in order to receive a dividend, then that is legitimate buying. If, after a time, he wishes to use his capital in some other field, and he sells his one hundred shares of stock, then that is commercial selling. If he gets a higher or lower price than he paid for the stock, then the difference is legitimate profit or loss. Stock exchanges originated undoubtedly to facilitate such transactions as these.

But as at present carried on, such trading as the above does not constitute *five per cent.* of the business done on the Stock Exchanges. Ninety-five per cent of the trading there is purely speculative, and has no relation to the investment demand for stocks.

Let us touch upon a few facts that may serve to throw some light on this point. Take the trading in two of the leading "pool" stocks, Sugar and St. Paul for instance.

The whole of the common stock of the American Sugar Co., is bought and sold on the New York Stock Exchange every six to ten days on an average *throughout the year.* There are only three hundred and sixty-nine thousand shares of the Sugar common stock, and yet, in fifty business days, between February 16 and April 16, 1898, *three million two hundred and twenty-three thousand three hundred shares of this same stock* were bought and sold on the floor of the New York Stock Exchange alone. The actual cash value of the Sugar Common stock traded in there on these fifty business days was about *four hundred million dollars.* If this rate of trading were continued throughout the year, *two billion four hundred million dollars' worth* of this one stock would be bought and sold on one New York Exchange. The total issue of this same stock is only *thirty-six million dollars.*

The peculiar thing is that no matter how many times the capital stock of this company has been bought and sold in the last four years on the floor of the Exchanges, there has been no change in the management of the Company.

And such manipulation of prices and betting on quotations is dignified by the name of "business;" and the managers of the game, the manipulators, are spoken of as "business men" and "eminent financiers," and "our well-known bankers and brokers." "It is a mad world, my masters."

The average number of shares of St. Paul common stock that is bought and sold *every month from one year's end to another*, equals twice the whole number of these shares. Do investors, those who carry their stocks for the dividends they yield, or for voting purposes, change their investments twice a month'?

Take another fact that throws light on the subject. There are about one hundred and thirty stocks traded in on the New York Stock Exchange. The year around two-thirds of all the trading will be confined to six or seven leading stocks. Some days manipulation in two stocks, Sugar and Tobacco, makes up two-thirds of the total trading.

Now if anyone can explain in the nature of things and as a result of a legitimate demand, why these facts are so; why for instance, less than one hundred shares of Chicago and Alton, a sound "Granger" stock should be bought and sold on a certain day, and on the same day *seventy-one thousand shares of St Paul*, a similar stock, should be traded in: and if furthermore, one will explain why about this same proportion continues in the trading of these stocks every day in the year; if we say, any one will explain this on *business principles*, then we will be ready to admit that the mass of trading in Wall Street is a legitimate, honorable business, governed by the same laws of supply and demand that control the trading in potatoes and cotton cloth. Until this explanation is made we shall adhere to our opinion that ninety-five per cent. of the business in Wall Street is part of a game.

We shall show later that it is

## NOT A GAME OF CHANCE,

but a game of skill.

Certificates of stock have no more value than waste paper except as they represent dividend possibilities or voting power in the management of the company. All buying and selling of stocks not based on these two features is simply betting on future up and down quotations. Ninety-five per cent. then of the business done on the exchanges is simply for the purpose of making up and down quotations for betting purposes.

We dwell upon this point at the outset because the public who play the game should understand that it is a game when they enter it. We shall show that the game has well-defined principles and rules that the public would do well to study.

The game is not a game of chance but a game of skill, directed by shrewd men who control millions of dollars. Just how much money can be commanded by the Sugar Trust Pool, for instance, we would not undertake to say.

It is not uncommon, as we have said, for from twelve to fifteen million dollars' worth of this stock to be bought and sold during one day on the New York Stock Exchange. While of course the Sugar Trust Pool does not do all the trading in their stock, yet it is evident that at all times the pool regulates and controls the price of this stock.

We think we are conservative when we say that the seven big pools that control the movements of the seven most active stocks on the exchange command a capital of not less than SIXTY MILLION DOLLARS in ready cash.

Sixty million dollars is a large sum you say to be put into any game. Who puts up the backing?

Of course the pool managers will not tell you this. But if you should guess that the "insiders" in the industrial and railroad companies whose stocks are manipulated by these pools, together with certain parties close to the management of our big life insurance companies; and also certain Wall Street banks, furnish a large part of the funds, your guess would not differ from that of some of the shrewdest observers in the Street. Certain it is that people who can command millions are the silent partners in the game.

Now capital is naturally conservative, and the larger the capital the more conservative it is. The shrewd capitalists who control these pools do not put their millions into a game of chance. The Wormsers, the Flowers, the Keenes, the Havemeyers, the Hoffmans and other pool managers, do not risk their own and their associates capital on an uncertainty. Far from it. Neither are they playing "give away."

These men absolutely control the game. They see the finish from the beginning, and they have the capital and the ability to reach the object they aim for in spite of the accidents and happenings that to the superficial observer seem to influence the course of the stock market. There is no chance but that these men will win, and hardly any chance but that the public, in the end, will lose.

There is no use, then, in mincing matters by calling a pack of cards a bundle of tracts. When in later pages you will have seen by the records how the movement of prices on the Stock Exchange goes through a certain well-defined course each year, you will be ready to acknowledge, we think, that human intelligence, and not chance, controls the course of the market, and that prices do not go up and down at haphazard as the public suppose.

If, then, ninety-five per cent. of the trading in Wall Street is purely speculative, a mere betting on quotations, and if the course of prices is controlled by a few shrewd minds, what kind of a game is it these men are playing? We know that the men who control the pools in Wall Street and who live in uptown mansions and belong to uptown churches think themselves to be, and wish the world to consider them, as "financiers." But before we are through we will show that these men and their silent partners are the managers of *the most stupendous gambling game* the world has ever seen.

It is a game where gains and losses are from one to two million dollars a day: a game that in New York City alone employs more than ten thousand smart men as brokers, clerks, and assistants.

A game that has its daily doings reported free of charge and at great length in every prominent newspaper in the country under the head of "Financial Markets" or "Wall Street Doings" or some other dignified heading.

A game where the "rake-off" to the brokers and the pools is more than one hundred million dollars a year, all of which must come out of the pockets of the public.

Does this latter statement seem extravagant?

Consider that there are eleven hundred members of the New York Stock Exchange and eighteen hundred members of the Consolidated Exchange. Not all are active members to be sure, yet on the other hand many of these men employ a small army of clerks and assistants in their offices.

Consider that last year *one hundred and forty-three million seven hundred and ten thousand* shares of stock were bought and sold on these two exchanges, par value of this stock was *fourteen billion three hundred and seventy million dollars*. Commissions on these transactions must have been a pretty sum.

Now trading one hundred shares of stock back and forth adds nothing to the intrinsic or dividend value of the stock, because such trading adds nothing to the earning power of the company whose stock is traded in. But at every trade the broker has received a commission, and in every ten trades ten commissions have come from somewhere and gone into the broker's pockets. Whose pockets do these commissions come from? They do not come out of the ground, as do the profits received from producing wheat and corn and coal and gold.

The broker's commission then must come directly from the pockets of the public who trade in stocks. These commissions are a "rake-off" in other words, and the public must lose what the brokers gain. But this is not all the public loses. There are three groups considered in the trading in Wall Street, namely the "Pools," the Brokers, and the Public. We have just shown that the brokers must get a very considerable sum each year. Now how much do the pools or insiders get in addition?

There is no way of estimating the amount the pools make each year, as far as we know. We do know that these men are shrewd and successful and are not there for their health. We believe that we were far within the truth when we claimed that the pools and the brokers together must take more than one hundred million dollars a year out of the pockets of the public.

Thus an amount equal to the total yearly loss by fire in the United States is annually swallowed up, as far as the general public is concerned, in "the game in Wall Street."

Isn't this a magnificent gamble then? All the Monacos and government lotteries in the world are not to be mentioned in the same day nor the same week with this game.

Consider these matters fully. Stock trading is unproductive. The farmer who sells his wheat, and pork, and cotton, gives the world something tangible for the money he gets. The miner adds something to the world's real wealth. The mechanic gives the world added power. The merchant has made it more convenient for the public to obtain the products of the earth. The professional man tries to remedy mankind's physical, or business, or spiritual ills. These men are engaged in legitimate businesses.

But the stock speculator adds nothing to the world's wealth. He is engaged in a betting or gambling game. He is simply a parasite. In the final analysis the rugged "granger" with his trousers tucked into his boots and his patched clothing, is a far nobler figure, and an infinitely more useful citizen than the smug "kings of finance" who manipulate the game in Wall Street.

We have no prejudice against stock speculation and the pools generally. We simply believe in calling a spade by its right name. We think, too, it is important, if you are to go into the game at all, that you should understand the character of the business.

We will presently tell you how to play the game, but before doing so let us consider for a moment what the losses in Wall Street mean. You should first consider your chances of a loss and what that loss will mean to you.

Do you ever stop to think how much ruin the yearly loss of one hundred million dollars spells to those who lose it? How much anxiety and despair to someone? How many sleepless nights? How many broken banks and broken hearts'? How many suicides' graves?

Those who have studied the subject know that there is no such prolific cause of suffering and despair in society to-day as is Wall Street and Chicago Board of Trade speculation.

Take the ruin caused by the Sugar Pool manipulation as an illustration. If one could get the statistics so as to know how many hundreds, yes thousands, of poor fellows have been crushed under the wheels of that Juggernaut Car it would be simply appalling. Every broker can tell you the names of scores who have lost everything betting on the flights of that "Will o' the wisp," "Sugar." We are not prejudiced against the Sugar Trust Pool. Their game is a nice little Klondike for us, as working on the "scale system" with a large margin makes us money easily and safely. We refer to this pool so frequently simply because it is the leading and the largest and most active pool.

The methods used by the other pools are the same in principle, and the ruin caused by them is as great in proportion to their size.

# HOW TO AVOID LOSS

How can the public avoid losing money in Wall Street? will be asked.

A good way for the public to avoid losing money there would be for it to keep out of the game.

We are afraid, however, that no warning will avail to prevent the public gambling in Wall Street, and therefore the only way to save the lambs is to show them some of the pitfalls in this business, and teach them some of the principles of play, so that as little loss as possible may fall upon these innocents.

Bear in mind, as we said before, that we are not taking ground for or against speculation. This is not a moral essay. We are simply giving you facts in cold blood, so that if you propose to trade in stocks you may know exactly what you are doing. You should clearly understand that you are entering a game, where, if you are not sharp, *your* hard-earned dollars will go toward the one hundred millions a year that is lost in the Street. If you lose your money you lose not that alone, but your health and your happiness as well. There is no business in the world that, win or lose, is so sure to wreck soul, mind, and body, as is Wall Street speculation.

# WHO TAKES PART IN THE GAME?

One might ask who does not?

We have a friend who had a broker's office in Washington. His firm had close connections with the Senate chamber. He assured us solemnly that more than half the senators at one time or another were the firm's customers. Whether his statement was true or false we do not know.

It was common talk both in the Street and in the financial and other newspapers when Mr. Cleveland was president that he speculated largely in stocks through his friend, Mr. C. E. Benedict, the broker. The large fortune Mr. C. retired with from the presidency is supposed to have been brought to him principally through Mr. B., from stock transactions. We have no opinion about this matter. We believe, however, that sooner or later the people will demand a law to prevent members of legislatures and of Congress from speculating in stocks, for the reason that every important question brought before Congress has a direct and oftentimes very large influence on the prices in the stock market. That the pools and trusts use Congress and our State Legislature, directly or indirectly, as aids in the game there can be no question.

After a very wide and cautious investigation we feel safe in saying that more than one-half the professional men in our larger cities try this game. We know that a still larger proportion of business men take a turn at it. To tell the truth we have never yet questioned *one man in well-to-do circles of business or professional life who did not admit knowing, by personal experience, something about this game.*

It is openly stated that there are more than seven thousand "bucket shops" alone run in this country, in addition to ten or fifteen thousand brokers' offices all outside of New York City, *all trading in quotations put out by the New York Stock Exchange and the Chicago Board of Trade, and all for the most part supported by the business and professional men of this country.* We may well ask who does not take part in this game?

Now then if after considering the above facts about this business you still desire to take a hand in it we will first call your attention to certain general principles, and then give you special rules that will aid you to play the game successfully.

# PART II.

One of the first things to notice is that only

## SEVEN OR EIGHT TRUMP CARDS

are used for the most part in playing this game.

Seven or eight stocks out of more than a hundred and thirty on the board contribute three-fourths of the transactions on the exchanges. You had better confine your attention to these and hold only these cards in your hand. These are the stocks that are manipulated by the big pools. If you will run your eye down the column of "numbers of shares sold" in the daily report, you will at once pick out the stocks that are handled by these pools.

For the last five years Sugar has been the leading card on the board. Tobacco at times comes next, and St. Paul is a good third; Burlington and Rock Island come next. Manhattan, Chicago or Peoples' Gas and Union Pacific preferred. All of these constitute the principal pool cards to-day. Time was when Atchison and Reading and Lackawanna and Missouri Pacific and other favorites were used; but these have been discarded for the most part, and the list given above are the ones to-day.

New cards may be taken up from time to time and old ones thrown aside, but take the year through only seven or eight cards are used as trumps, and *nine-tenths of the transactions* will be in these particular stocks. Toward the end of the campaign, either on the bull or bear side, the outside stocks will be made use of more prominently.

To succeed you must study the manipulation of the pool cards. Confine your transactions to these.

# POOL STOCKS AND SPECIALTIES.

As we have said there are six or eight stocks handled by the big pools; the rest of the stocks may be called "specialties."

Should one deal in the pool stocks or the "specialties?"

At the beginning and during the first half of both the bull and bear campaigns, stick to the big pool stocks. These stocks are the first to move and will make by far the most rapid progress up or down. These stocks are the leaders, the active fighters, both in the advance and the decline, and the others are the reserves.

When Sugar and the "Grangers" have advanced ten or fifteen points the "specialties" will be up only three or five. When, however, the leaders are near the top then the laggards come up with a rush and a hurrah. Invest in the leaders first, then with the profits made in them you can make a turn in the "specialties" later in the campaign. Don't invest in anything that is not active as shown by the volume of daily transactions.

There are certain good stocks that while not exactly specialties are late movers: Missouri Pacific, Louisville and Nashville, and Western Union are such stocks. When after a week's advance you see Missouri Pacific suddenly get active and come charging up you may know that, for the present, there will be a rest and a reaction in the leading stocks; and when late in the campaign, either on the bear or the bull side, Missouri Pacific becomes *very* active and makes a big move, then you may be sure the end is not far away. This is a never-failing sign. Missouri Pacific is the "Black Horse Cavalry" that gallops to the front to cover the retreat of the leaders.

# THE POOLS.

We find many people who are disposed to doubt our statement that the pools direct and control the grand movements on the stock exchanges. We shall show later by our diagrams that every year movements in the stock market are the result of deep laid plans, and that the general direction of prices follows a course or chart laid out six months or a year in advance. *We shall show that the same or similar plans are followed year after year*, and that the close student may form a tolerably accurate idea of what the general direction of the market will be for a period of time.

It is not claimed that one can tell just how prices will move for any particular day by this study, but one will learn the object the pool managers are aiming for, and as these men control ample capital and are the shrewdest financial generals in the world, one may feel sure that their campaign will be brought to a successful termination sooner or later.

# A CAMPAIGN.

Any person who takes a broad view of Wall Street speculation will be struck by the resemblance between the campaign in the Street each year and the course of a war campaign when directed by some great general. Take a "bull campaign" as an illustration.

There are at least two campaigns each year in the street, a bull and a bear campaign. The bull campaign begins after the bear campaign has been brought to a successful close. The bull campaign begins when prices are low, when the general public are bearish. All the news at such times seems to favor a decline. (The pools can manipulate news and newspapers as well as prices.) There are wars, or rumors of wars; there are foreign complications; there are high money rates, and general dullness. There are numerous clouds in the financial sky. Yet if one notices closely, he will see that after these conditions have existed for some time, the prices on the Stock Exchange, in spite of the continual bad news, do not go any lower. The prices fluctuate day by day up and down over a narrow range, but for some reason, in spite of the continued short selling of the chronic bears, the decline is checked. Although there is no advance in the market and may not be for weeks the bull campaign has already commenced.

At these times the pool generals are quietly and steadily mobilizing their forces. In other words *they are accumulating their stocks* and locking them up in their strong boxes.

These men act on the principal that the time to buy stocks is when prices are low; and the time to sell is when prices are high. The pools buy when times are bad, and sell when everything looks good. *The bull campaign begins in gloom and ends in glory.* It begins at the *bottom* and ends at the *top*.

When this period of low prices that we have mentioned has lasted two or three months and the pools have secured their stocks, the word is given out to commence the advance. A battle takes place, the bears are defeated, and prices advance. Then there may be a retreat to encourage more short selling. Again an advance takes place and this time it goes a little further. So the contest wages, the prices going up and down, but on the whole advancing. Finally toward the end of the campaign, after four or five months of gradually advancing prices, the advance begins to be rapid and continuous, the bears are then routed "horse, foot and dragoons," prices are booming, the public, and even the bears, are madly buying, all the news and indications are favorable for a continued advance, *the volumes of transactions are very heavy*, and right then – the bull campaign ends.

Take the course of prices in the year 1897 as an illustration. In the Winter and early Spring, St. Paul and Burlington, for example, were selling under 70, and sugar at 110 to 112; other stocks in proportion. Those were dark, dull days and the bears seemed to have everything their own way. For three months prices moved up and down sluggishly over a narrow range. The public were decidedly bearish. At this time we published that Sugar, which was selling then at about 112, would sell as high as 137 in the summer. We drew this from the study of the records of the fluctuations of this stock. Of course we were laughed at. In May the advance commenced and continued slowly and steadily. Up and down prices went, but each month saw them a little higher. Take the high and low prices of Burlington from April to October as an illustration.

|        | April. | May. | June. | July. | Aug. | Sep. |
|--------|--------|------|-------|-------|------|------|
| Low,   | 69     | 72   | 77    | 81    | 87   | 96   |
| High,  | 73     | 77   | 85    | 89    | 99   | 102  |

By the middle of September both St. Paul and Burlington were selling at 102, an advance of 30 points, and Sugar was above 155. (We venture to say that the very people who were on the short side of Sugar at 112 in the Spring, and laughed at our prediction then, were on the long side at 150 in August, and predicting that the price would go to 175. It went to 109 instead.)

Those were bright days last fall and everyone was bullish; yet that was the end of the advance. Why?

Because the pools who bought St. Paul and Burlington around 70, and Sugar around 110, when things looked bad, sold out at an advance of from 30 to 40 points in these stocks when things looked good. Could there be any better explanation for the sudden ending of the advance?

Whatever the excuses and reasons put forth for the check in the upward movement in prices last Fall, the real reason was that, in the early Spring the pool held the stocks and the public was short. In the Fall the public held the stocks and the pools took the short side of the market.

The course of prices in 1897 was not an exception but the rule. In 1896, "Presidential Year" there were two distinct bull campaigns and two bear campaigns. The first bull campaign commenced in

January and ended in June. The second commenced in August and culminated in November.

As a rule there is but one bull campaign and one bear campaign each year and approximately speaking each campaign lasts six months.

This is one of the most important facts to remember if you are thinking of embarking on the stormy sea of Wall Street speculation. We do not mean that each bull and each bear campaign will last just six months to a day. We do not mean that a campaign will commence and end at exactly similar dates each year. We are laying down principles and general rules now so that, by their aid, you can study the philosophy of speculation for yourself.

Take the history of prices on the Stock Exchange for the last year and a half to make this point clear.

The first week in November, 1896, prices reached top. Now in March, 1897, after a six months' decline, they were dragging on the bottom, bobbing up and down, but making no further decline and likewise no advance.

In April, 1897, prices began to sneak up. When did they get to the top? About the middle of September, or, practically speaking, in about six months. From this time on prices declined and in February, 1898, another six-month period, they struck bottom and dragged along on a low level until about the last of April. At the present writing, May, 1898, they have commenced an advance that ought to culminate in September or October this year. Leaving out 1896, which, on account of its being a Presidential Year, had two distinct campaigns, you will find that prices on the Stock Exchange have gone through similar movements to those mentioned above every year for the last twenty years.

An examination of the course of prices for the last four years, starting after the panic of 1893, will show this:

1894, Low point was in March; high point in August
1895, Low point in March; highest in September.
1896, two distinct campaigns; campaign No. 1, Low point in January; high point in June. Campaign No. 2, Low point in August; high in November.
1897, Low point in April; high in September.
1898, Low point in March; high ——?

From this you will see that all these campaigns but one lasted about six months.

Bear in mind as we said before, that you cannot lay down a hard and fast rule in this matter. There are exceptions to all rules and there are, to a certain extent, exceptions to this. But if the following pages and especially the records are carefully studied, you will get suggestions that will aid you in judging the trend of the market so that you will know when to keep out, when to take the bull, and when the bear side.

We will give you a hint now, based on the preceding statements.

### HINT NUMBER ONE.

After prices have been *declining for four or five months* and then come, comparatively speaking, to a standstill, simply moving up and down over a narrow range, *do not be tempted to take the bear side of the market.* Everything will look bad at such times. The financial papers and the brokers will all be bearish. There will be every apparent reason why stocks should be sold short, but *don't sell.* Depend upon it the next marked move in prices will be upward.

The pools at such times are accumulating stocks and they aim to buy without putting up prices. They buy quietly and slyly. High rates for money does not deter them, as they can pay for their stocks and lock them up. The worse the outlook the more the bears sell and the cheaper the pools get the stocks. After two or three months of such trading the pools decide to open the campaign and then the advance begins.

How shall one know when the advance will commence? This question will be answered now and is

## HINT NUMBER TWO.

After the market has gone on for some time in the manner above mentioned, *there will come a day or two of almost complete stagnation in the market*. Perhaps only fifty or sixty thousand shares of stock will be traded in on the exchange. Everyone will be talking of "the deadly dullness of the stock market." *Then you can buy stocks with safety and hold them for a good rise.*

On April 27 of this year (1898), the stock market had become so dull that only seventy-two thousand shares of stock were traded in on the New York Stock Exchange, and half that amount on the Consolidated Exchange.

We said then that the advance would commence in a few days and we advised our friends to buy stocks to hold. Within two days the advance was under way, and in a week the average trades on the New York Stock Exchange alone amounted to three or four hundred thousand shares a day.

For several weeks previously the price of St. Paul had been moving up and down between eighty-four and eighty-seven. On the 27th the price was still eighty-five. The next day it opened at eighty-five and began to rise. On May 9 the price of St. Paul was ninety-six and seventy-one thousand shares of this stock alone was traded in on that day.

In ten business days the price of this stock had advanced eleven points. In the same length of time Sugar had advanced eighteen points, Rock Island sixteen points, Burlington & Quincy twelve points.

"Oh," but it will be said, "this advance was due to a special cause, Admiral Dewey's victory at Manila."

The *rapidity* of the advance was due to this cause, but not the advance itself. The real cause was that the pools had been buying the stocks for two months and were ready to advance prices.

The same phenomena, namely, a period more or less long of nearly stationary prices, then a day or two of dullness and *almost complete stagnation* has preceded every bull campaign for the last ten years to our knowledge.

The explanation of this phenomena is simple enough. As has been said, the pools have bought stocks and the bears have been selling them for weeks. The bears at length got tired of selling them. When they stop there are no more trades. Of course then there comes stagnation, followed by a rising market.

## HINT NUMBER THREE.

If it is important to know when to enter the market on the bull side it is just as important to know when to get out and take the other side.

We have hinted at this in the explanation that "a bull campaign begins in gloom and ends in glory." We mean that the bull campaign ends when prices are rising rapidly, and the volume of daily transactions is enormous. The volume of transactions should put one on his guard.

After five or six months from the time when stocks were at the lowest point, after there has been a good advance and now the bull market is under way with great enthusiasm, then there will come *three days of rapidly advancing prices all along the line with great excitement and an enormous volume of business*. The universal cry is "now we have an old-fashioned bull market," and there is an unanimous scramble for stocks; this marks the culmination of the campaign. The pyramids of stocks that have been built up on the bull side are ready to tumble and great will be the fall thereof. Remember this advice applies only if the bull campaign has lasted five or six months after prices touch bottom. At such times sell out and go into the country to cool off. If you are near the scene you will be hypnotized by the enthusiasm and tempted to make one more turn on the bull side.

Now to illustrate the truth of "Hint Number One" and "Hint Number Three" by statistics. Read those hints again and then consider the following facts.

For two months before the bull campaign of 1897 commenced (the months of March and April), there were in round numbers eight million shares of stocks traded in on the New York Stock Exchange. This was at a time when prices were low and the pools were quietly accumulating stocks.

Six months later the transactions on this same exchange for the months of August and September amounted to about twenty-five million shares, worth at par two billion five hundred million dollars. This was at a time when prices were high, and the public were obligingly taking the stock off the hands of the pools at an advance of twenty to forty points.

# ACCUMULATION – DISTRIBUTION.

The whole philosophy of the game in Wall Street is summed up in two words.

The pools first accumulate stocks. We have explained when and how they do it.

Having accumulated they must hold on and gradually manipulate the prices upward. They cannot unload on the public suddenly or the prices would tumble before the stocks were peddled out. It takes a month or two after prices have been worked up near the top to get the public to take the stocks off the hands of the pools. The public have to be stimulated to buy by all the means known to shrewd managers.

As a rule the public has more money and consequently more courage in the *Fall* than in the Spring, and, hence, as a rule, the bull campaign *begins in the Spring and ends in the Fall;* when the public take the stocks.

As we said before, the pools after accumulating the stocks must put the prices up and *hold them up* until they can get out.

They must use the financial columns of the press, market letters, business and crop reports, every artifice that will tend to put a bright outlook before the public. Then the pools can distribute their stocks. When once this distribution has taken place nothing can prevent prices from sagging. Increased earnings of railroads, glowing reports of crops are still put out. Slowly at first, but surely, the tide goes out. After a time the news and reports that were erstwhile so roseate, seem to be a little doubtful. Bills will be introduced into Congress that threaten to interfere with railroad traffic or to unsettle the currency. These bills are introduced by the agents of the pools and are not expected to pass. They have the intended effect, however. The pools' financial papers are used at this time to spread distrust as to the future of the market. The financial columns of the daily press reflect, mirror like, these views; and so after some months prices will be brought down to the point where the pools can begin to accumulate stocks again.

Such a movement as this *must take place every year of necessity.* If the market kept advancing all the time prices would in a year or two be literally "out of sight." Prices must come down so that the pools can buy again.

Do not understand, however, that the prices will necessarily come back on the decline to the low points of the previous year. Since 1893, most stocks have been and still are on the up grade. Every year sees both the low point and the high point higher than the previous year.

This is particularly true of Sugar stock, as will be seen from the following illustration:

|       | Low.                      | High.        |
|-------|---------------------------|--------------|
| 1894  | $75 Feb.                  | $114 Aug.    |
| 1895  | $86 Jan.                  | $121 June    |
| 1896  | 1st campaign $79 Jan.     | $125 June    |
|       | 2nd campaign £95 Aug.     | $125 Nov.    |
| 1897  | $110 April                | $159 Sept.   |

The country itself has been on an up grade since 1893, and the pools have taken advantage of that fact in arranging their plans of campaign.

The lowest point reached is not the accumulation point, or the price at which the pools buy the most of their stock. On the final break when the pools bring the stocks down to where they can afford to gather them in, the downward rush carries prices temporarily below the buying-in price.

And in the final upward rush, at the end of the bull campaign, the price is carried temporarily above the distributing point. This will be seen on an examination of the records of the fluctuations on a later page.

# ACCUMULATION AND DISTRIBUTION.

This is the keynote of the movements of the prices on the Stock Exchange. When once this point is clear in your mind all the mysteries will become plain to you. The game in Wall Street is a

GAME OF HUMAN NATURE.

The pool generals are men who study crops and politics, both domestic and foreign, and legislation and finance. They know when the time is ripe to start a bull or a bear campaign, and when they can afford to end it. They know when natural conditions will warrant an extended movement, and, on the other hand, when only a moderate one will be accepted, and they lay their plans accordingly. They take a long look ahead; they study all these facts, but specially they study human nature. They play upon the hopes and fears of the public through their agents of the press and on the exchanges and in the legislative halls, as the organist plays on his instrument. It is not a difficult game for them to play so as to win *with the means they have at their command*. The cards they use are both "marked and stacked," and they take no chances. They can use, and must use, the same tactics to a great extent each year, because the principles of the game must of necessity be always the same, *Accumulation and Distribution*. Beside, there is not much need of their changing their plans and traps, as the speculative public is so short-sighted that the same bait can be used year after year. On a later page we will give a diagram entitled "Sugar traps," that will illustrate this point.

Now that the principles underlying the game are understood by you, we will give some practical hints that will enable you to be as safe as it is possible to be in playing this game.

# SPECULATION: A SCIENTIFIC STUDY.

One ought not to play this game at haphazard. One ought to make as careful a study of it, if he plays at all, as the expert whist player makes of that game. One ought to keep a record of the movements in prices of the big pool stocks, the ones whose transactions are the largest day by day in the manner mentioned, and illustrated further on in this work. This record will tell what the pool in any particular stock is doing. "Actions speak louder than words," and the fluctuations in price are a record of the acts of the pools.

The pool generals do not, as a rule, take the public into their confidence. Personally we would not believe any statements they might make as to the course of prices, simply because we have too high an opinion of the shrewdness of these men. While they might and do at times give a true "tip," yet the "outsiders," who get these "tips" and profit by them once or twice or three times, will be brought low in the end. The "tips" to buy will be profitable at the beginning or middle of the bull campaign, but *still stronger "tips" to buy will be put out at the end*, to aid the pools to unload on the public, and then all that has been made by taking the previous "tips" together with the original capital will be lost. The very fact that the first "tips" were good will give one confidence to "plunge" in the last fatal "tip."

While on the subject of "tips" we wish to say that we have no confidence in those advertising tipsters who for ten or twenty dollars a week will tell you the names of stocks that are going to move ten or twenty points up or down.

The whole thing is absurd. If they know so much why don't these fellows trade for themselves and make their own fortunes. It is guesswork on their part, while you take the risk in the trading and pay for the guessing. Furthermore we happen to know that these forecasters are often used by the pools. The pools give them certain true "tips" at first only to be able to use these tipsters to fool the public with in the end.

But if, as we have said, you keep an accurate record of the fluctuations in prices, and remember that these fluctuations are not due to chance but are the result of design, you will have a fairly good idea of what the pools are doing. These records are circumstantial evidence. Now if you will act with the pools, irrespective of what the general public is doing or saying, you will be on the safe side.

If it seems to you too much trouble to keep records and to study this subject, then you have no business in it. It requires study and time and patience to make a success in a mercantile business or in a profession, but it seems to be the general opinion that anyone can rush into stock speculation and make a fortune. Stop and think a minute. If this theory were true, if the amateurs could win as a rule, or if even one-half of them could win, there would not be any game in Wall Street in two years. If the public in general should take away more money from the Street than it brought, who would pay the expenses of the game? Someone must lose, and if it were the brokers and the pools they would shut up shop after a season or two. If you are not to be one of the losers, then you must be smarter than your neighbor or the public in general; you must look further ahead. You must get in when the majority think prices are going down, and you must get out when they think the market is going higher. Remember that every time you sell one hundred shares of stock there must be some person with like aims and hopes as yourself to buy it. The "clearing house" does not buy your stock, nor does the "market." When you buy a hundred shares of stock you do not buy it for its dividends, or to leave it to your grandchildren, but to sell again at an advance. The fellow who buys from you also expects to sell it at an advance, or at least he thinks the price is going higher. The party who buys from him expects the price to advance. No one will buy if he thinks the price is going down. Now if you expect to unload your purchase you must sell when the public want to buy. If you hold till the price goes to what you think is top, and the general public think as you do, no one will be foolish enough to buy your stock. Prices cannot go up all the time. As a matter of fact the records show that in the course of a year the price goes down as often as it goes up. Someone must be left with stocks on their hands bought at top prices each year. See to it that it is not you. This is a game of "beggar your neighbor. " In Wall Street it is you against your neighbor, wherever and whoever he may be, and you must beat him to win. This is the cold-blooded truth about the game, and if you have any sentimental compunctions against playing such a game you had better keep out of the Street.

# PANICS.

The one fear that haunts the mind of the amateur trader in Wall Street is panics. A few words on this point may not be amiss.

A real, thorough panic comes only once in about twenty years. Witness 1837, 1857, 1873, 1893. After a panic such as 1893, there will be two or three years of uncertainty and then confidence will be restored and the financial barometer will commence to rise. Between each big panic there are about two smaller cycles, or distinct periods of prosperity, followed by depression. A period of prosperity and advancing prices lasts about three years. Then the pendulum swings the other way and prices gradually decline for four or five years.

We are now in the era of increasing good times and advancing prices, commencing from the spring of 1897. The high point for prices on the stock exchanges will be higher each year than the preceding high point until top prices will be reached, probably in 1899.

The following diagram gives a very good idea of the ebb and flow of prosperity.

It will be noticed that the big panic years each commenced after the top of a rise (Nos. 1, 3, 5, 7, 9), and one of the smaller rises at that. It will also be noticed that the period of prosperity that followed a panic reached a higher level than the preceding period of prosperity (Nos. 2, 4, 6, 8, 10). It will also be noticed that this period was not followed by a real panic but by a decline, while the second period of prosperity preceded a panic.

## PANICS

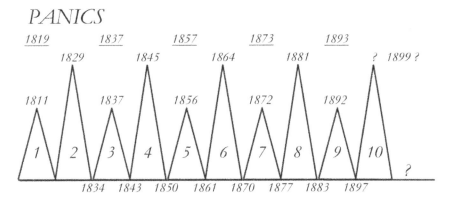

History will repeat itself just as long as human nature remains as it is. Panics are a disease of the public mind. There was just as much sunshine and rain and good land and good crops, and just as much money, and the same men and women, in this country in the years 1893, 1894, and 1895 as in the three years preceding the panic. Nature's condition had not changed; the change was in the public mind.

Short-sighted people attribute panics to some particular cause, such as tariff laws, or Clevelandism, or the Gold Standard, or Free Silver, or Free Trade agitation.

The cause lies deeper. The above are only the foam of the wave. The real reason for panics is in the character of the American mind; the American tendency to rush to extremes; to carry prosperity into inflation, and inflation to what is called a "boom."

Then there comes the inevitable collapse of the iridescent soap-bubble in the form of a panic.

There will be no panics in the business world, even small ones, for several years at least from this date; and no large panics for fifteen or twenty years.

# PANICS ON THE STOCK EXCHANGE.

There will be no panics in the stock market except artificial ones for many years. *But every year when the pools want to buy back stocks an artificial panic will be gotten up.* Take the present year for instance. There was a panic among the speculators over the outbreak of the Spanish-American war. Was there any reason for it? Did any sane man believe that such a war would injure this country? Did the panic extend to any other line of business than the stock market? We did not hear that there was any panic among the holders of New York real estate, or owners of bank stocks at the time.

But prices of stocks, good dividend railroad stocks, tumbled as if the country was on the verge of ruin. What proved that this was an artificial panic was the fact that prices began to advance as soon as war was declared and have been steadily advancing ever since while the war continues.

*There are no panics on the stock exchanges except when the pools are out of stocks.* When the pools have the stocks there can be no panic, for the real owners of stocks can lock them up and take them off the market. Stocks then are as firm as real estate. The above is our theory and the facts seem to accord with it.

When a bull campaign is commenced you will be safe from panics if you keep on the long side of the market with a good margin. If you are trading in stocks on a small margin you will be liable to panics every day.

When the pools sell out then you should be working your system on the short side and in that case you need not fear panics, but rather welcome them.

Every big fall in prices that we have noticed on the exchanges has not come until after a big rise.

We give our theory for what it is worth. So far as the records go it is correct. What the future may bring forth we do not know, but we take it that human nature does not change materially from century to century.

# FLUCTUATIONS.

A study of the fluctuations or records of the daily ups and downs in the prices of stocks furnishes the key to an understanding of this whole business.

Take any of the big pool stocks and you will notice that the price at which a certain stock is selling changes from a dozen to a hundred times a day the year through. Now the intrinsic or dividend value of this same stock may not change for years.

Sugar Common is a noteworthy illustration.

This stock has paid its three per cent dividend in each quarter since the beginning of 1894 as steadily as the seasons succeed one another. The real or dividend value *has not changed one dollar a share for four years*. But the selling price on the exchanges has not been thus constant. The price in actual sales varies every hour the year through on an average more than one hundred dollars on each hundred shares of stock, or three million seven hundred thousand dollars an hour on whole number of shares. In 1897 Sugar stock sold at one hundred and ten dollars a share in the Spring. A few months later at one hundred and fifty-nine dollars; then still, a few months later, at one hundred and ten dollars again. The latter price being in the Spring of 1898. Yet during the whole twelve months of changing prices it was the same old Sugar stock, earning and paying its regular dividends, and really worth as much at one time as another.

Between these extremes there were how many *thousands* of fluctuations in the price do you suppose?

Were these fluctuations a matter of chance or was there design running through them all?

While the large majority of the small variations may undoubtedly have been partly due to the struggles of the three thousand brokers on the two exchanges to scalp a profit out of each other on the changing quotations, yet when you take a broad view of these changes you will see that a master-hand, or head rather, controlled the fluctuations, and led the price through seeming chaos to a predetermined end.

If you know anything about the Sugar Trust Pool you know that the "insiders" had it in their power to put the price from $110 to $159 in six days instead of taking six months to do it as they did. But the Sugar Trust people were not born yesterday. Mr. Havemeyer and his friends prefer to milk their cow (the public) rather than kill her. By manipulating the stock market carefully and with patience, they not only get their regular twelve per cent. per annum dividends, on refining sugar but they also get two hundred per cent. per annum from the pockets of the speculative public.

Now you can see what the constant fluctuations in the prices of the pool stocks mean. These fluctuations are the smoke and dust of battle that hides the plans of the general from the men in the thick of the fight. Turn to the records of the one-half point fluctuations in sugar on last pages, and see if we have misrepresented or misjudged the Sugar Trust Pool and their methods. You will see that there are hundreds of fluctuations around a certain low point. This was the laying of the foundation of the building; the greater the number of fluctuations near the bottom the higher the building, that is, the higher prices go.

The movements of all the pools as shown by the fluctuation records are similar to those of the Sugar Trust Pool. A study of the fluctuation record of St. Paul and Burlington is particularly interesting, and we refer you to their records.

# SYSTEM IN SPECULATION.

Many "Sure and safe systems" for playing the game in Wall Street have been advertised from time to time.

Most, if not all, of these systems seem plausible enough until one looks into them carefully. Then weakness will be found.

Every system if it is worthy of the name of a system at all, must be absolutely automatic and machine-like, that is, the one working it must have no opinion about the market, or at least he must not let his opinion influence his actions. If he begins to be guided in his transactions by his views as to the future course of the market then he ceases to follow a "system" and is guided by his judgment. Again, a "system" to be "safe" must be safe at all times and in all emergencies. "A chain is no stronger than its weakest link." If a system is to be followed it must be absolutely safe so that one can venture his last dollar if necessary without fear of losing it.

After a pretty careful study of the different systems put forth we are of the opinion that unless one has almost unlimited capital every system will break down at times, unless one uses some judgment in directing and managing it. In other words, no "system" is to be absolutely and solely relied on by the man who has only a moderate capital.

In our opinion a "system" should be the engine that does a certain work and does it economically and safely. *But every engine requires an engineer, or, at least, an intelligence, to start it in the right direction and stop it at the right time.* Someone who knows when to send it ahead and when to reverse it. So it is with speculative "systems" in Wall Street. We believe that every amateur should follow to a certain extent a "system" in trading, but he should use his judgment in directing that system. That is, *"system" and brains must go together.*

There are undoubtedly several good systems if rightly handled. An Irishman once applied to us for advice to get him out of a difficulty. We told him that there were two or three plans by which he could be relieved. Quick as a flash he said:

"Try the *best* one first, sor, and if that succeeds we'll not need the rest."

So in our remarks about "systems" we will discuss the one we think to be the best for amateurs first, and then may not consider the others at all.

The "Simple Scale System" is our preference. The "Scale System" means simply buying or selling a certain number of shares of stock at every point or half-point up or down as the prices advance or recede, and then taking profits on every individual transaction when the profit shows. We will explain this more fully on a later page. Now for the dangers of this "system" when one relies on it fully without using his brains.

Suppose A says, "I will buy one hundred shares of St. Paul at every point up or down from a certain price, and sell each purchase at a point and quarter advance, so as to net one hundred dollars profit on the transaction. After any one hundred shares of stock is sold out, if the price recedes to the original buying price, I will buy again."

Suppose he commenced this "system" last fall in September, and bought his first one hundred shares of stock at par; bought another one hundred at one hundred and one, sold the first one hundred at one hundred and one and one-quarter, and then as the price touched one hundred and two bought another hundred. Then if you will look on the records you will see that the prices went down. He buys at par again, at ninety-nine, at ninety-eight, and so on down to ninety-six. Then, the price advances and he sells out such lots as show a point and a quarter profit and has a good profit on these. But the price goes down again and continues to go down until by March 15 he will have sixteen hundred shares of St. Paul on hand, some bought at one hundred and two. At this time he will have had to put up a margin of twenty-eight to thirty thousand dollars with his broker to protect these purchases. Of course he made many hundred dollars' profit on the fluctuations meantime. Now when St. Paul goes back on the next bull campaign, all his purchases made on the decline will show him splendid profits. But there are two points to consider here.

Suppose his broker should fail when the market is at bottom. What becomes then of his chance to get back his twenty-eight thousand dollars. Suppose the market should continue to decline. Or suppose that St. Paul should suspend paying dividends for a time as Missouri Pacific did, when it was selling at eighty-four, and like Missouri Pacific go down ultimately to ten dollars a share; how much margin would have been required in that case? This is the weakness of the "scale system," or any other system worked, as we have said, automatically and without using intelligence.

Now on the other hand suppose A had commenced buying St. Paul on the "scale system" in the *Spring* of 1897, instead of the *Fall*, when the price was around seventy and the bull campaign was just commencing. If he had bought his one hundred shares of St. Paul at seventy and again at seventy-one and so on, taking advantage of the fluctuations to buy back the shares sold out at a profit, by fall he would have had some thirty thousand dollars profit. Thus the system if started right would have been safe and profitable at all times until the end of the bull campaign. Now having worked this "scale system" on the long side of the market during the bull campaign, at the end of that time if he could have reversed the system, turned his engine around, and commenced selling short every point up or down until the Spring of 1898, he would have had another twenty-five thousand dollars profit, and been safe at all times.

This so called "scale system," with *brains to direct* it is the safest and most favorable plan the amateur can follow, if he has only a moderate capital to work on, and we unhesitatingly recommend and advise it. So long as one knows the general trend of the market and goes with it, he need never fear any ups and downs if he has a sufficient margin at the start.

Let us make this system so clear that even a child can understand it.

The first requisite is to select one or two good dividend-paying, active stocks, that is, one or two of the big pool stocks.

The essential thing is to first determine, as we have said before, whether a bull campaign or a bear campaign is in progress, so as to know whether to start your system on the long or short side of the market.

We have tried in the preceding pages to give you suggestions for determining in which direction the market will go. Having settled this point in your mind put in your orders to your broker.

Let us suppose, for instance, you started the "scale system" on the long side of the market in Bock Island in April, 1897.

You send your broker an order as follows:

"Buy me ten Rock Island at market (say sixty-five) and ten more every point up or down. Hold only one lot at a time at any particular quotation.

"Sell each purchase one and one-half points advance. Buy back at original buying price any lot that has been sold. Continue until further orders."

Now this order is very comprehensive and covers the whole ground. Your broker buys ten shares at sixty-five: the price advances and he buys ten more at sixty-six: then the price declines and he buys ten more at sixty-four. As he already has ten at sixty-five he does not fill the order again there. At sixty-three he buys ten more shares. Now the price advances to sixty-five. He sells the lot bought at sixty-three at one and one-half points profit. Each purchase, remember, *is to be treated by itself as if it was the only lot of stock you had in the market.* Now the market declines again, he buys ten shares a second time at sixty-three and ten more at sixty-two. Then the market turns and advances to sixty-six. As it goes up he sells the lots bought at sixty-two, sixty-three, sixty-four, each at one and one-half points profit, and you still have the lots bought at sixty-five and sixty-six. Take a paper and pencil and work this out as given above. You will see that you have closed five transactions at a net profit on the closed transactions of about seventy-five dollars and you still have two transactions open, one of which shows you a profit of ten dollars and the other is even. Now the price advances to sixty-nine and your broker buys at sixty-seven, sixty-eight, sixty-nine, but he sells meantime three lots each at a profit of fifteen dollars.

Of course if you knew beforehand that the price was going down to sixty-two and then up to sixty-nine, you could have waited till it touched sixty-two before buying and then waited until it got to sixty-nine before selling, and thus have made a very large profit. *But you cannot know beforehand just what the market will do.* All you can determine is the general trend of the market, and, knowing this, the "scale system" will make your transactions safe at all times if your margin is fair, and will make a steady profit. The more ups and downs, the more profits you round up. So long as it is a bull campaign and you are working this system on the long side of the market you are safe, no matter how great the fluctuations.

In May, 1897, Rock Island played all the month between sixty-one and a half and sixty-six and a half, moving up and down frequently. In June the price fluctuated up and down, finally getting to seventy-six. In July it wobbled up to eighty-three.

In August to ninety-seven; and in September to ninety-seven.

Now this "scale system" as given above was always in the market: you always had stock to sell on every advance and on every decline your system bought.

The proper time to buy is when the prices decline and the proper time to sell is when the prices advance. The amateur, working by guess, usually sells on the decline and buys on the advance.

The profits in the six months' working of a "scale system," between April and September, 1897, would not have been less than one hundred per cent. on five hundred dollars, and the system would have been absolutely "safe" during this time. Most of the time your broker would not have needed more than one hundred dollars to protect your transaction. All the time too your profits taken in would have been increasing your margin. In order to be absolutely safe, however, you should have had five hundred dollars at least up with your broker at all times, and then your trades would have been protected even through a ten point straight fall, something that will never occur in a good dividend paying granger stock after the bull campaign has commenced.

You have now, let us say, worked the "system" on the bull side up to September 1, 1897. The hints given you in the preceding pages tell you that the end of the bull campaign cannot be far off. You can wait a while and when you find that the market is getting top-heavy, turn your system around and commence selling on the short side of the market, every point up or down. No matter if it goes against you two or three points, it will come back again. In giving your orders to the broker in working the "scale system" on the short side of the market, simply substitute the word *sell* where the word *buy* occurs in the preceding order.

It will require nerve to turn your "system" at the end of the bull campaign, for the press, and the public, and the brokers, and the "tipsters," will all be against you at this time. Remember, however, that when the pools have sold out, stocks must go down sooner or later, no matter how favorable general conditions may be for an advance.

All this requires some intelligence on your part. Well, it requires intelligence to make money in any line of business, and this is as true or truer in Wall Street than in other places. An extract from a circular just received contains some very pertinent remarks on this point.

"A great many unreliable brokerage firms are flooding the country with catchpenny literature of how to make a fortune in three months with a one hundred dollar investment, and similar fairy tales, which although ridiculous on the face of it, still often deceive the innocent, and frequently rob quite intelligent men and women of hard-earned savings or inherited fortunes. No money is ever made easily, and if speculation is so easy, why do not these men speculate themselves instead of asking for your cash. Why, if speculation was so easy – nobody would work; but the truth is, it is extremely difficult."

We have thus given you a safe and conservative plan or "system" to work on. If the amateur will follow it he or she (for unfortunately many women are engulfed in this whirlpool of speculation) will be safe at all times and make money. It is the only system that we can conscientiously recommend to amateurs, as it is simple and safe.

A study of the records of the actual fluctuations in some of the active stocks given on a later page, will show what one could have made by such a system. Of course the "system" can be modified. For instance, if one has a large capital he can give the following order: "Buy ten Rock Island at market and double the quantity bought on each point decline."

Thus at sixty-five you buy ten: at sixty-four you buy twenty: at sixty-three you buy forty: at sixty-two you buy eighty. Now a turn of a point and a half sells out the eighty shares at a profit of one hundred and twenty dollars on that transaction alone, and even if you close now, your other stocks are evened up; but if you hold as you should, a further advance to sixty-five gives you another one hundred dollars profit.

This system will work all right if you have *plenty of capital and you are on the right side of the market.* Without these two essentials the system will break a millionaire.

Are you willing to study the business and work on a safe system, getting from five per cent. to fifteen per cent. a month on your money?

*Not one speculator in a thousand will be satisfied with any such profit or will stick to a safe "system " of this kind.* The ordinary speculator wants to start with a capital of from two to five hundred dollars and double and treble and then quadruple it each month. But in trying to do this his little pile goes, sooner or later, to make up the hundred million dollars that must be lost yearly by the public in Wall Street.

A capital of five hundred dollars is little enough to start the "scale system" on ten-share lots.

This "system" must be worked on the Consolidated Exchange rather than on the New York Stock Exchange, for one cannot deal economically in small lots on the latter exchange.

A capital of a hundred thousand dollars is the lowest that should be used in any "system" on the New York Stock Exchange, dealing in one-hundred-share lots. As we are not brokers and have no interest in either exchange, we are giving unprejudiced advice in this matter. Avoid the one-hundred-share-lot transactions unless you have unlimited capital.

Thus having given you what we have found to be the best system and the safest for amateurs and one that we believe to be used by the pools themselves to a considerable extent, after a campaign is well under way, it will not be necessary to discuss any other "system."

# THE OUTLOOK.

At the present writing (May 1898), there is every evidence that we are to have a phenomenal advance in prices this year.

War is the biggest kind of a bull factor. Inflation of prices always accompanies a war after it is thoroughly under way. The government is expending millions of dollars daily; the present crisis has united all parties and we need have no fear of socialistic legislation in Congress: the farmers have not been so prosperous in twenty years: the biggest wheat crop ever known is before us with the certainty of good prices for it; *but more important than all* we have just recovered from the depression that followed the panic of 1893, and *are in the cycle of advancing prices* that always follows a panic.

Our records show that the accumulation point of St. Paul this spring was about eighty-eight. This is more than ten points higher than the accumulation point a year ago. We have no hesitation in prophesying that St. Paul will sell the present year at one hundred and fifteen or better.

Burlington ought to go still higher.

Sugar was accumulated around one hundred and sixteen and if the Sugar Trust Pool follow their usual tactics they will put the price *very high* before the campaign is over. A glance at the records of the wild gyrations of that particular gamble ought to warn the amateur against trading in that stock except in small quantities.

The whole market is in for a wonderful advance and *new records of high prices and large volumes of transactions* will be made this year. The heart of every chronic bear will be broken before this campaign ends.

A word to the wise is sufficient.

We have been asked before now why there were two distinct bull and two bear campaigns in 1896, when there is usually but one grand up and down campaign each year.

A moment's reflection ought to give the answer.

The summer of a presidential year is always a time of uncertainty and doubt and prostrated business.

The summer of 1896 was bound to be a bad one. It was a question as to whether Free Trade or Protection, Free Silver or the Gold Standard, would be the policy of this country for the coming four years.

The pool generals, as we have said, are far-seeing men; they started the bull campaign in January instead of waiting until April as usual. By May they had the prices at the top and were unloading steadily all through May and the first part of June. Then came the political conventions, and then the usual course of the market after the pools had sold out. By August prices were back to where they were the preceding January and the pools took hold for a second bull campaign, which was short and sharp and ended in November.

# PART III.

## HIT OR MISS HINTS.

### HINT NUMBER FOUR.

GREED and impatience are the causes of most of the losses in Wall Street.

A man puts a thousand dollars into a Real Estate loan and is contented to wait a year to get sixty dollars for the use of his money. This same party will go into Wall Street with a thousand dollars and expect to make two or three or five hundred dollars a week on his capital. Of course he usually loses. By studying the principles laid down here and working on a "scale system" with plenty of reserve margins he can with safety make five per cent. to ten per cent. or fifteen per cent. a month on his capital. This will not satisfy the speculator, however. One hundred per cent. a month is the least that will content him.

An old book, not greatly in vogue in Wall Street, says somewhere, "A fool and his money are soon parted." Solomon would have no difficulty in understanding from whose pockets must come the one hundred million dollars a year that is lost by the public in the street.

The one thing essential for success then, *after you understand the principles laid down in this work*, is that one should not overtrade. If you are carrying too much stock for the amount of your capital, a two or three-point decline in prices makes your broker call on you for more margin, and you are compelled to sell at a loss. If you are right in your views as to the general course of the market you should buy more stock on the decline, instead of selling. If you do this, within a day or two prices go up again, and then what promised to be a loss turns out to be a profit. If you work on the right side of the market, starting with a ten or fifteen-point margin so that you can buy more on reactions, you will not need to take a loss during the whole campaign.

## HINT NUMBER FIVE.

This is very important. *As a rule do not sell stocks on the third day of a decline* (unless you are working on the "scale system") and *do not buy on the third day of a rise.* We cannot explain why prices move practically three days in one direction and then react, but this is the case. There seems to be about two waves a week, one upward and one downward. If it is a bull campaign the upward wave will be longer than the downward, so that the tide gradually creeps in. If it is a bear campaign the downward wave will be longer than the upward, and the tide gradually recedes.

## HINT NUMBER SIX.

After stocks have advanced three days and close at top and open high the next morning there is almost sure to be a reaction of a point or two.

*After they have declined three days and close at bottom they are almost sure to advance the next day.*

In a bull market when you are waiting to get in on the reactions do not wait any longer than two full reaction days. On the third morning commence buying on a scale. Sometimes the market reacts only a little, *simply resting for two days* after its rise.

This will be the time when conditions, such as cheap money and business confidence, are favorable.

At these times buy on the *third day* of the resting period.

## HINT NUMBER SEVEN.

In a bull market the largest volume of transactions are on the advance. The reactions are marked by smaller volumes. The reverse of this is true during the bear campaign. Closely watch the volumes of transactions and they will give a true indication as to the trend of the market.

## HINT NUMBER EIGHT.

During a bull campaign never try to make a turn on the short or bear side of the market. No matter how straight the information may be that a reaction is due, do not allow yourself to get on the wrong side of the market for a day. You may succeed three or four times in cutting out a profit on the short side at such times, and then the next time you try it the market will run away from you and wipe out your margins.

*If you wish to be safe* stick to the bull side during a bull campaign. If you think there is going to be a temporary reaction then sell out if you like and wait for the reaction, and commence buying again. Do not go short.

During the bear campaign do not go long of the market, even for a time. If you think a rise is due, wait for the rise, and then commence selling short on a scale up. The market must come back sooner or later.

## HINT NUMBER NINE.

If you start in at the beginning of a bull campaign it is a good plan to "pyramid" for a time, that is, hold your purchases and add more stocks as the prices advance and your margins grow. For instance, you buy fifty St. Paul at eighty-five, and fifty more every two points up for a rise of ten points. Your profits are then fifteen hundred dollars. If you study the St. Paul fluctuations in the records on a later page, you will see that once or twice in the year St. Paul makes a move of this kind.

In order to succeed in this you must commence at the beginning of the bull campaign. At a later stage more money will be made by playing the "scale system" so as to take advantage of the reactions.

## HINT NUMBER TEN.

We advise studying two or three pool stocks closely. Keep accurate records of their fluctuations and movements. After a time you will be able to read the minds of the managers of these pools.

## HINT NUMBER ELEVEN.

Do not let London quotations influence your views as to the course of the market.

## HINT NUMBER TWELVE.

After any decided general rise of six to ten points with *great excitement at the close of the advance,* then even if the market is ultimately going higher, the advance will stop for a time, and, of course, there will be more or less reaction. There will then be a number of up-and-down fluctuations, extending over two or three points in the grangers and more in the industrials. (See fluctuation record.) In other words we might say that the market after such a rise has had a "gorge" and must wait to digest its meal. Here is a time that the "scale system" picks up the profits. Here is the time, too, that "scalping" gets in its best work.

The same law holds true of a sharp fall in prices.

## HINT NUMBER THIRTEEN.

The "tips" and "points," and "they say" and "we hear," and the "gossip" of so-called financial papers, as well as the letters of advertising brokers, ought not to be allowed to influence your views as to the course of the market. If these "tips" agree with indications furnished by your records, well and good. If not, pay no attention to them. In the long run one will be safer and make more money if he does not read the financial papers and financial gossip.

## HINT NUMBER FOURTEEN.

One must take broad views and look ahead, in order to succeed in Wall Street. There everything is anticipated. If bad news is expected, do not sell after the worst is known, but buy. If favorable news is looked for, buy in advance, and sell out when the good news becomes a fact and is known to the public. Anticipate. The public said, "If war is declared then we will sell out and take the bear side of the market." All the pools had sold out long before and were waiting for an opportunity to get back their stocks. Prices began to *go up* as soon as war was declared.

If you wait until the uncertainties are all removed and the clouds all gone from the financial skies before buying, then prices are up ten to thirty points and those who "anticipated" are ready to unload on you. If you sell when the worst has been told and hope is dead then the pools are ready to buy, because a change is at hand. In Wall Street as in Nature:

"It is darkest just before the dawn."

Anticipate! Anticipate!! Anticipate!!!

## HINT NUMBER FIFTEEN.

Keep away from the brokers' offices and do not watch the "ticker." To succeed in Wall Street one must form independent judgments and have the courage to act on his views.

Now if you are hanging around a broker's office listening to the talk and opinions of the "Wall Street Wrecks," who congregate in such places, your mind will be influenced by such talk in spite of yourself. The "ticker" is the worst thing you can study. When prices are rushing up, the "ticker" whispers, "buy, buy;" when prices are going down a panic seizes you if you are watching the "ticker," and you sell when you should buy instead.

The "scale system" buys and sells exactly contrary to the whisperings of the "ticker."

The only amateurs who make money in Wall Street are those who keep away from the brokers' offices.

## HINT NUMBER SIXTEEN.

Keep large margins. With a capital of one thousand dollars it is not safe for the amateur to trade in more than twenty-share lots of two or three good stocks. It is for this reason that we advise the amateur to work through the consolidated rather than on the New York Stock Exchange. Unless one is a desperate gambler he cannot afford to work one-hundred-share lots of stock with a smaller capital than from five to ten thousand dollars. Work on the "scale system" and trade on the Consolidated Exchange if your capital is moderate.

## HINT NUMBER SEVENTEEN.

"Second tops and bottoms." Mr. O. B. Greene, a very shrewd broker, has put forth a theory that has considerable truth in it. We will state this theory in his own words and just as published.

"When a market has gone through the stages of quiet and weak to active and declining, then on to semipanic and panic (causing extremes on unexpected news beyond the power of any one to anticipate) Watch for the day to arrive when Volumes of transactions Increase Largely over all preceding days. You will find purchases made at previous low Chart records or on a Scale Down on This Day on Ample Margin will bring very profitable results contrary to appearances or what your judgment advises. Should you wish to act more conservatively. Wait until the Large Volume Day Closes, showing a reaction of a few Points from bottom figures. Do Not Fail then to send orders immediately to Buy on the next or second

Downward Movement At Or Near the lowest previous bottom figures touched on the first downward movement of the large volume day. You will observe the Greater the Volumes and the Bear Excitement the more certain of the lowest figures being touched a second time. Then purchases should be made without relying on lower quotations because you will not be able to buy from this point on a scale down for the reason that on the second decline prices seldom go over a few fractions below first lowest movement before a strong advance sets in.

"The reverse is true on an upward movement of the same character.

"RULE TO OBSERVE.

"At this Time You Must Lose Your Individuality and become an Automaton, Paying No Attention to News Gossip, and Act on the Second Movements.

"Nerve and Patience is needed.

"These purchases should be held for marked advances because excited Bull movements Always follow on the heels of Bear movements in Proportion to the extent of the Volumes and Excitement at the extreme decline."

There is much truth in this suggestion, and this truth applies to both the selling and buying movements accompanied by great excitement and large volumes. We indorse everything Mr. Greene says on this point unhesitatingly, but in acting on this suggestion we caution you to keep the campaign in mind. If it is a bear campaign and you buy for a turn do not hold for too big a reaction.

**HINT NUMBER EIGHTEEN.**

Don't let your desires influence your judgment. The usual speculator if he is long of stocks can only appreciate arguments on the bull side of the market.

The chronic bear has his eyes shut as to the most patent signs of a bull market.

In both cases the desire or hope blinds the judgment.

There is no room for partisanship or politics or patriotism or religion in stock speculation, any more than there is in a game of whist or chess.

A habit of keeping the records of the fluctuations will soon teach one that this is a game of skill based on the eternal laws of human nature.

Do not however, neglect a study of natural conditions and the way they may influence the public mind. The pool generals do not neglect these facts.

## HINT NUMBER NINETEEN.

There are always one or two leaders even in the big pool stocks. The leader or leaders start first and get to the top first, and then are unloaded on the public while the other stocks are advancing. The one that gets to the top first will be the first to start on the downward course. Remember, however, that the price usually makes top a second time before going down and the price must fluctuate up and down just below the top for some time.

During the bear campaign the leaders will get to the bottom and begin to rise while the slower ones are tumbling. There will be second bottoms as well as second tops. Study your chances and while stocks are coming down rapidly wait until the second bottom on big volume days.

## HINT NUMBER TWENTY.

Don't be either a "chronic bull" or a "chronic bear." It ought to be plain to you from the preceding pages and from a study of the diagrams and records that there is a time to take the bull side of the market, and a time to take the bear side. You should change about every six months, when the pools change.

If you must be a "chronic," that is, a person on the same side of the market the year around, stick to the bull side *for the next two years*. It is far better, however, to go with the tide each year.

## HINT NUMBER TWENTY-ONE.

As a general rule get on the bull side in the late Spring and stay there until Fall. Then reverse and take the bear side. There is usually, however, after a decline in the Fall, a small bull campaign, *starting about the middle of December and lasting till the middle or latter part of January.* Then a decline until April, when the grand yearly campaign starts. This is a general rule, but your records if carefully kept will be your best guide.

## HINT NUMBER TWENTY-TWO.

A bull campaign may be divided into three periods.

> 1st Period. – A sneaking bull market.
> 2nd Period. – A creeping bull market.
> 3rd Period. – A final grand rush.

The first upward move in the campaign comes as a surprise to the bears and the public.

Everything has looked so favorable for lower prices, there were so many clouds in the financial sky, that the sudden advance in prices is looked upon as a temporary move only. "The market was oversold," is the cry, and nearly everyone expects it to go back to the old prices again. After the bears have recovered from their confusion they commence putting out short sales, the bull leaders draw back a little to encourage them, and there is a slight recession in prices, sometimes equal to half of the advance.

Then comes the second period – "a creeping bull market." Here the pools take hold of one stock after another in succession, or one or two at a time, and advance them without any excitement and only a moderate amount of business. Many stocks are quiet during this period, some may recede a little temporarily, but from week to week the prices creep up. There is no excitement during this period. There are many plausible reasons put out to show that prices should go down at least a few points. One of the most prominent financial papers every year tells the public at this period that "there is going to be a bull market later, but it will start from a lower level," and so the public wait for reactions that do not come. The public at this time is very suspicious; they do not really have confidence in the bull market until prices are up twenty to thirty points and rapidly advancing. A rather dull market with one or two stocks at a time advancing and the public waiting for reactions to get in, or selling short to average up past losses, are the characteristics of the second period in the bull campaign.

Then comes the third period, "the final grand rush," the "old-fashioned bull market," fortunes made in a week – on paper: rapidly advancing prices all along the line; specialties and outsiders, "wild-cat and red-dog stocks" galloping to the front; great excitement; an enormous volume of daily transactions and then—

## WHAT COMES NEXT?

Well you ask your friends who loaded up with stocks in September, 1897, and November, 1896, and September, 1895, and September, 1894, what came next in their experience.

## HINT NUMBER TWENTY-THREE.

On a dull advancing market after the foundation for a bull campaign has been formed, do not play for reactions. If everyone is waiting for reactions so as to buy back short stocks, or to start in on the bull side "from a lower level," be sure there will be no material reactions. *What everyone expects does not happen in Wall Street.*

Play the active stocks one after another as they commence to move. Remember the pools have got to put prices up and hold them up before they can unload.

## HINT NUMBER TWENTY-FOUR.

A bear campaign is not so easily characterized as is the bull campaign.

After the big excitement at the close of the bull campaign there is of course a sharp reaction and then prices rush up again to make a second top. Then there is a dull, slow, sullen retreat in prices. The public who have bought stocks at the top, grit their teeth, put up more margins with their brokers and hold on. Hope springs eternal in the human breast: but during the bear campaign prices sag and sag until hope gives way to despair. After about three months of the sagging market, generally in late December or in January, there is a bull campaign lasting four or five or six weeks, and then a still further decline until the real period for accumulating stocks, which will be shown by the records of the fluctuations.

The bear campaign offers as many and as safe chances for making money as the bull campaign, some years better chances, but, as we have said before, for the next two years we will be in the cycle of advancing prices and the advances will greatly exceed the declines.

## HINT NUMBER TWENTY-FIVE.

When you have seen any stock lay a broad foundation for a rise, as shown by the records of the fluctuations, and then this stock advances *beyond the former stopping point of each advance, accompanied with large volumes of transactions*, you may be sure that this particular stock is in for a big rise. The height of the rise may be measured by the breadth of the foundation. Govern yourself accordingly.

Remember that fluctuations mean something. They are the result of design not chance.

## HINT NUMBER TWENTY-SIX.

During the bull campaign, stocks generally sell lowest for the week on Thursday afternoon; on Fridays and Saturdays they advance and reach top either on Monday or Tuesday morning. In the bull campaign buy Thursday night and Friday morning; sell Monday and Tuesday morning. Reverse this rule for a bear campaign.

# CONCLUSION
# BY CLEM CHAMBERS

It is amazing that so little has changed in the stock market in 130 years.

This book was the first ever published with a stock chart, one that is quaint but in effect revolutionary. (You'll find the charts reproduced at the end of this edition.)

However, for all the change over the years, the key thing that hasn't changed in the market is human nature and it is human nature that drives the market. The underlying game laid out in this book is still being played today. As in other sports, the clothing and equipment may have changed a bit. The players' facial hair is different, the scale of the audience has ballooned, even a few rules have been amended, yet the dance itself is little different.

The game might be faster, but the score lines remain recognizable.

You probably could not write this book today as the modern examples would get you sued. As such, when you read this book you should map it onto what you see today in the markets.

You might not believe that conspiracy and manipulation could exist on this level in the modern world. But it does. It's even bigger.

Today the US Federal reserve is pumping $85 billion dollars a month into the US economy, or rather into US assets' values. It is the biggest manipulation and conspiracy of all time. It may turn out benign, it is most certainly legal, but the markets have never been so rigged.

We do not have the ability to do anything but coattail this manipulation and I can attest there has been a lot of money to be made care of the manipulation and conspiracy that is QE.

So from the Fed at the top of the world order, the hedge fund talking its own book or tweeting its latest stock buy, to the penny stock pumper at the dubious bottom of the markets, they are all on a mission to push markets their way.

If you can simply avoid the consequences of playing the game by spotting the field marks of the game itself, that is a boon. Losses are negative profits, so avoiding them as you invest ends up the same as making money.

However, if you insist on being drawn towards the flame, it helps to know what happens next.

There is however one last thing. You are reading this. This means you are keen to learn the markets. As in any skill game, the more you know and the more you practice the better you will get. Read twenty good books on market theory (but please, none on how to trade yourself to wealth) and you will be amazed at how little people who trade and invest know. The newspapers, the pundits, financial advisers will all start sounding like fools.

This is the real trick to making yourself wealthy from stocks. If you read one **boring** investment book (I hope that won't disqualify my books, but the more technical and colorless the book the better) a month for the rest of your stock market investing career, you will be highly successful.

Simply by avoiding the pitfalls of a market heavily tilted towards gamblers, you will set yourself on the right course for solid long term profits. Make no mistake, while a minefield for the uninitiated, the stock market is the only place a normal man with diligence, determination and grit can take small sums and turn them, over the long term, into significant wealth… not by gambling on *The Game on Wall Street*, but by understanding it.

# MARKET DICTIONARY.

BEAR. – A believer in lower prices.

BLOCK. – A large number of shares bought or sold in one lump.

BREAK. – A quick small decline.

BULGE. – A quick small advance.

BULL. – A believer in higher prices.

CLIQUE. – A combination of a few operators to control the fluctuations of a certain stock.

COVER. – The buying in of grain or stocks to fill short contracts is called "covering."

DIVIDEND. – That part of the earnings of a stock which is apportioned to each share, thus a 2 per cent. dividend is $2 on each $100 worth of stock.

DROP. – A decline in values largely due to natural causes.

EX-DIVIDEND. – A stock so sold does not include or carry to the buyer a recently declared dividend, but the dividend goes to the seller or former owner.

GRANGERS. – Those railroads which handle principally farm products, the following are usually included in this classification; Burlington, St. Paul, Bock Island, Northwestern, and Atchison.

HOLDING THE MARKET. – Buying enough stock to keep the price from declining. Such buying is often called "Supporting."

INSIDERS. – Those who own a controlling interest or an important interest in the stocks of a concern, and who are therefore influential in directing its affairs. Insiders are closely watched by the public, as their transactions often shape the market.

LIMIT. – A set figure at which one's trade is to be made or closed.

LONG. – One who has bought for an advance.

LONG INTERESTS. – The aggregate amount of investment holdings in any speculative market.

MARGIN. – A part payment deposited with your broker to protect against loss. Your margin must always more than equal the loss shown by your trade.

OUTSIDERS. – The general public. Those who invest in stocks or grain on their judgment as to the general situation.

POINT. – In stocks a point is one dollar per share. In grain one cent per bushel.

POINTER. – A theory or fact concerning the market for a given stock or grain on which a speculation is based.

POOL. – The stock and money contributed by a syndicate to control the price of a given surety.

PROFESSIONALS. – Those who make speculation, usually of a scalping nature, their daily business. They rarely buy stocks to hold, but trade in and out every day.

PYRAMIDING. – Enlarging one's operations by the use of profits which one has made. For instance, if one buys 5,000 bushels of wheat and the market advances 2 cents he sells, realizes $100 profit, and with this in addition to his original margin he buys 10,000 bushels of wheat, which he closes on a further advance and makes a still larger investment. On steadily advancing markets with reactions of not over 2 to 4 cents this plan makes large profits, but must not be followed too far, and liberal margins should be kept.

SCALPING. – Buying and selling on small fluctuations of the market. Taking a small profit or a small loss.

SHORT. – One who has sold for a decline.

SHORT INTEREST. – The aggregate amount of short sales in any speculative market.

SLUMP. – A severe and unexpected decline.

SPECULATION. – Buying commodities not needed for use, or selling commodities not owned, with the hope of making profits by fluctuations in the values of these commodities. A speculator buys wheat because he hopes to sell it at a better price, but not because he needs it for use. He sells Sugar stock because he believes he can buy it at a cheaper price later, and make the difference.

STOP LOSS ORDER. – An order to close one's trade at a given point in order to stop loss.

TRUST. – A combination of the various manufacturers of a given article to control its production or sale, as the Sugar Trust, the Leather Trust, etc. The life and success of these trusts depend upon the legality of their combination and their ability to control the trade in their merchandise, and to resist competition therein.

# SUGAR TRAPS

The contempt of the Sugar Trust Pool, for the memory and understanding of the speculative public, is shown most strikingly in what we have designated as "sugar traps" No. 1 and No. 2.

The diagrams there given are the actual records of the movement in prices in Sugar stock on the dates mentioned.

## TRAP NUMBER ONE, 1895.

Sugar stock had been accumulated by the pool around ninety; then for four or five months the price had been gradually advanced until it reached one hundred and nineteen; then for six weeks the price had been manipulated up and down over a range of three or four points, during which time the pool unloaded on the public; then on the 17th it sold "ex-dividends," and then came the fatal June 20. During the three following days sugar fell eight full points, then rallied three points, and then during the next three days fell another eight points. The total fall was from one hundred and nineteen to one hundred and six, or thirteen points between June 20 and June 28, 1895.

## TRAP NUMBER TWO, 1896
## (JUST ONE YEAR LATER).

Sugar stock had been accumulated by the pool around par; then for four months the price had been gradually advanced until it reached one hundred and twenty-five ; then for seven weeks the price had been manipulated up and down over a range of about four points, while the pool unloaded on the public. Then the stock sold "ex-dividend" on the 17th; and then came the fatal June 20. During the next three days Sugar fell ten full points, then rallied three, and then in the next three days fell eight points more. The total fall was from one hundred and twenty-two to one hundred and eight, or fourteen points between June 20 and June 28, 1896.

Are any comments necessary? Compare the two diagrams and notice the remarkable similarity of the two traps.

Are these movements results of chance, or is there design manifested? "What fools these mortals be," to be caught twice by such a trap as this. Warned by the experience of 1895, when the same movement started on a similar date in 1896, how much could one have made by selling short two or three hundred shares at about one hundred and twenty, and then after the three days fall and the rally, putting out two or three hundred shares more for another three days fall?

Notice the second bottoms made after each fall.

The same game was not played on the same dates in 1897, because the advance did not commence in that year until the middle of May, and of course the price was not worked up to the unloading point by June.

# THE ANNUAL GRAND CAMPAIGN OF THE SUGAR TRUST POOL.

The accompanying diagram gives an outline of the plan of operations that has been carried through by this pool since 1893; a glance will make the whole matter clear.

At the accumulation period, and during the first half or two-thirds of the advancing period there are always points out to sell Sugar short. One year the talk is that Congress is going to pass laws that will hurt the trust; another year it is the State Legislature that injure it; at all times there are sure points out that the Arbuckles or some other big company are going to start opposition refineries and thus affect the Sugar stock. These points and tips are circulated industriously in the Winter, Spring and early Summer, and the speculators seem to have an insane idea that the proper caper is to sell Sugar short.

Now glance at the records and see what has actually taken place in the price of this stock every year.

There has been a time each year when one should sell it short; there has also been a time when one should *not* sell it short.

Who inspires the news bureaus and the tipsters to give out the tips to sell sugar short? Is it possible that the Sugar Trust Pool itself is smart enough to use such tools? We think so; "everything is fair in love and war," and Wall Street.

## NOTE.

The method of keeping the records of the fluctuations in the price of stocks as shown on the charts in this book is as follows:

Suppose St. Paul sells at 85 then goes to 86 and to 87. Then the price turns and reacts to 85 again. Then it turns again and goes to 86, 87, 88, 89. Then reacts to 87. Then goes up to 90 and down to 89. The record should be made each day in the order in which the changes occur,

|     |     |     |     |     |     |
|-----|-----|-----|-----|-----|-----|
|     |     |     |     | 90  |     |
|     |     | 89  |     | 89  | 89  |
|     |     | 88  | 88  | 88  |     |
| 87  |     | 87  | 87  |     |     |
| 86  | 86  | 86  |     |     |     |
| 85  | 85  |     |     |     |     |

the corresponding quotations should always be on the same horizontal line.

A little study and practice will soon make it an easy matter to keep this record.

Mr. W. P. Eager, a very intelligent broker on the Consolidated Exchange, has made an exhaustive study of the fluctuations in the leading pool stocks for the last six years.

We give here his results on Sugar and Burlington:

## SUGAR.

| Year. | Fluctuation. | | High and Low. | Number of Shares Traded. |
|---|---|---|---|---|
| 1892 . . . . . . . . . | 375 | Points | 115 3/8–78 1/2 . . . . . . . . . | 4,371,100 |
| 1893 . . . . . . . . . | 750 1–2 | " | 134 3/4 – 62 . . . . . . . . . | 10,589,100 |
| 1894 . . . . . . . . . | 603 7–8 | " | 114 7/8 – 75 3/4 . . . . . . . . . | 12,936,700 |
| 1895 . . . . . . . . . | 491 | " | 121 3/8 – 86 1/2 . . . . . . . . . | 10,050,500 |
| 1896 . . . . . . . . . | 517 1–4 | " | 126 5/8 – 95 . . . . . . . . . | 9,794,800 |
| 1897 . . . . . . . . . | 567 5–8 | " | 159 1/2 – 109 1/8 . . . . . . . . | 9,097,500 |
| | 3,305 1–4 | | | 56,839,700 |

## BURLINGTON.

| Year. | Fluctuation. | | High and Low. | Number of Shares Traded. |
|---|---|---|---|---|
| 1892 . . . . . . . . . | 246 5–8 | Points | 110 5/8 – 95 . . . . . . . . . | 2,710,200 |
| 1893 . . . . . . . . . | 428 1–8 | " | 103 7/8 – 69 1/4 . . . . . . . . . | 2,828,500 |
| 1894 . . . . . . . . . | 278 1–2 | " | 84 1/8 – 68 5/8 . . . . . . . . . | 3,059,900 |
| 1895 . . . . . . . . . | 267 1–4 | " | 92 5/8 – 69 . . . . . . . . . | 3,114,900 |
| 1896 . . . . . . . . . | 372 3–4 | " | 83 3/4 – 53 . . . . . . . . . | 3,528,300 |
| 1897 . . . . . . . . . | 327 1–2 | " | 102 1/4 – 69 1/4 . . . . . . . . . | 5,784,000 |
| | 1,920 3–4 | | | 21,025,800 |

"The fluctuations and volume referred to have been recorded in the New York Stock Exchange, 1892 to 1898. Now then, – there are several other exchanges whose total volume of sales run well into the millions of shares each year. Furthermore, the above startling total fluctuation would be *more* startling if it were possible to get at the *actual* fluctuations. For instance, HIGH and LOW on Sugar, for a given day, might show a fluctuation of 2¼ points, and the total fluctuation might have been nearer five points.

"As a conservative estimate the writer considers that ⅓ of 3304 points Sugar fluctuation, ⅓ of 2377 points Gas fluctuation and ¼ of 1920 points Burlington fluctuation for six years should be added to arrive anywhere near the actual fluctuation.

"Thus you will note a fluctuation of certainly over 4400, 3300 and 2400 points in Sugar, Gas, and Burlington respectively, during the past six years."

# PRICE CHARTS

## PRICES OF RAILROAD AND MISCELLANEOUS *STOCKS* IN NEW YORK–*1896*.

| STOCKS | January Low High | February Low High | March Low High | April Low High | May Low High | June Low High |
|---|---|---|---|---|---|---|
| Chic. Burl. & Qu. | 71 ¼ – 78 ⅝ | 76 ¾ – 81 ⅞ | 73 ⅝ – 78 ¼ | 77 – 82 ⅝ | 77 – 81 ⅛ | 72 ¾ – 80 ⅞ |
| Chic. Mil. & St. P. | 63 ½ – 72 ½ | 71 ⅝ – 79 ⅝ | 73 ⅝ – 78 ⅜ | 74 ¼ – 79 ½ | 76 – 79 ½ | 73 ⅝ – 79 ⅛ |
| Chic. & No'west. | 94 ⅞ – 100 ½ | 99 ⅝ – 105 ¾ | 101 ⅜ – 104 ½ | 102 ¾ – 106 ¾ | 104 – 106 ½ | 100 – 106 ¼ |
| Chic. R. I. & Pa. | 62 – 69 ⅝ | 69 – 74 ⅞ | 68 ½ – 73 ½ | 70 – 73 ¾ | 69 ⅛ – 72 ¼ | 65 ¼ – 72 ⅝ |
| Louisv. & Nash. | 39 ⅞ – 47 ¼ | 45 ½ – 55 ⅝ | 48 ⅜ – 54 ¼ | 48 ¾ – 53 ¼ | 48 ¾ – 52 ⅝ | 47 – 53 |
| Missouri Pacific | 22 ⅜ – 26 ¼ | 20 ⅞ – 25 ½ | 22 ¾ – 25 ¼ | 23 ⅞ – 29 ¾ | 24 – 28 ¾ | 19 ⅝ – 25 |
| Northern Pacific | 2 ⅜ – 5 | 4 – 5 | 1 ⅜ – 4 ¾ | 1 – 1 ¾ | ¼ – *5 ⅝ | *2 ¾ – ‡9 ½ |
| Pref . | 10 ⅛ – 16 ⅛ | 14 ¾ – 17 ⅝ | 10 ¾ – 17 ½ | 10 – 13 ⅛ | 11 ¾ – *15 ¾ | *13 ¾ – †17 ¼ |
| Union Pacific | 3 ½ – 7 ¼ | 6 ¾ – 9 | 6 ⅛ – 8 ⅜ | 7 ⅞ – 10 | 7 ¼ – 8 ⅜ | 6 ½ – 8 ⅝ |
| Am. Sugar R. Co | 97 – 108 ⅜ | 106 ¼ – 118 ⅜ | 113 ½ – 117 ¾ | 116 ¾ – 126 ⅝ | 120 – 125 ¼ | 109 ⅝ – 125 |
| Am. Tobacco Co. | 74 ¾ – 84 ¼ | 75 ½ – 83 ¼ | 71 ⅜ – 90 ⅞ | 67 ¼ – 95 | 62 ⅝ – 72 | 61 ½ – 68 |
| Chicago Gas Co. | 62 – 67 | 63 ¾ – 70 | 64 ½ – 68 ⅝ | 67 ¾ – 70 ⅜ | 66 ½ – 70 ⅜ | 61 ½ – 69 ⅝ |
| Gen. Electric Co. | 22 – 29 ⅜ | 27 ½ – 33 ⅝ | 30 – 39 ½ | 36 ¼ – 38 ¾ | 33 ½ – 36 ⅞ | 27 – 34 ⅝ |
| West. Union Tel. | 81 ½ – 85 ⅝ | 82 ⅞ – 87 ¼ | 82 – 85 ¾ | 83 ¼ – 87 ½ | 84 ½ – 86 ½ | 82 ⅜ – 86 ¾ |

\* Trust receipts; 1st instalment paid.  † 2nd instalment paid.
‡ 3rd instalment paid.  § Trust receipts; all assessments paid

| STOCKS | July Low High | August Low High | September Low High | October Low High | November Low High | December Low High |
|---|---|---|---|---|---|---|
| Chic. Burl. & Qu. | 62 ½ – 73 ½ | 53 – 66 | 60 ½ – 71 | 66 ¾ – 77 | 76 – 83 ¾ | 68 ½ – 79 ½ |
| Chic. Mil. & St. P. | 66 ⅝ – 76 | 59 ⅞ – 69 ½ | 65 ½ – 73 ⅞ | 67 ½ – 74 ½ | 73 ⅝ – 80 | 70 – 75 ¾ |
| Chic. & No'west. | 92 ¼ – 101 ½ | 85 ¼ – 96 | 95 – 100 | 96 ⅜ – 103 ⅜ | 102 ½ – 106 ¼ | 100 ¼ – 106 ⅜ |
| Chic. R. I. & Pa. | 52 ½ – 66 ¾ | 49 ¼ – 56 ¾ | 55 ⅜ – 63 ⅝ | 57 ⅞ – 67 ⅛ | 67 – 74 ⅞ | 64 – 70 ¼ |
| Louisv. & Nash. | 42 ¾ – 49 ¾ | 37 ¼ – 44 ⅞ | 38 ⅞ – 44 ⅛ | 41 ¼ – 48 ⅛ | 47 ¼ – 53 ⅜ | 45 ⅛ – 51 |
| Missouri Pacific | 15 ⅛ – 21 ¾ | 15 – 17 ⅞ | 17 – 21 ½ | 18 ⅜ – 22 | 21 ½ – 26 ⅛ | 18 – 22 ⅞ |
| Northern Pacific | †5 ½ – 8 ½ | ‡3 ½ – §10 ⅝ | §9 ⅞ – 14 ⅝ | §12 ½ – 14 ¾ | §14 ¼ – 16 ⅞ | §12 ½ – 15 ½ |
| Pref . | †12 ¼ – 17 | ‡10 – 18 ⅛ | §17 ½ – 22 | §18 ¾ – 22 ½ | §22 ½ – 28 ⅝ | §21 ⅜ – 25 ¼ |
| Union Pacific | 5 ¾ – 7 ⅛ | 4 – 6 ⅛ | 5 – 7 ¼ | 5 ⅞ – 9 ¾ | 9 – 12 ½ | 8 – 11 ½ |
| Am. Sugar R. Co | 100 – 111 ½ | 95 – 108 ⅞ | 107 ¾ – 117 ⅝ | 105 – 116 | 115 ¾ – 125 | 108 – 117 ⅝ |
| Am. Tobacco Co. | 55 – 62 ¾ | 51 – 60 ⅞ | 58 ⅛ – 67 ¼ | 60 ⅜ – 76 ½ | 74 ⅜ – 84 | 73 ¼ – 80 ½ |
| Chicago Gas Co. | 49 ½ – 63 ¼ | 44 ⅝ – 54 ¼ | 53 ¾ – 63 ¼ | 57 ¼ – 71 ½ | 71 ⅜ – 78 ¾ | 70 – 77 ¼ |
| Gen. Electric Co. | 20 – 27 ⅝ | 21 ⅛ – 25 | 23 ½ – 29 ½ | 24 ½ – 29 ½ | 29 ¼ – 35 ½ | 29 – 33 ⅞ |
| West. Union Tel. | 77 – 83 ⅞ | 72 ¾ – 79 ½ | 77 – 84 ⅞ | 81 ½ – 86 ⅛ | 85 – 90 ¼ | 80 ⅞ – 87 ½ |

\* Trust receipts; 1st instalment paid.  † 2nd instalment paid.
‡ 3rd instalment paid.  § Trust receipts; all assessments paid.

PRICES OF RAILROAD AND MISCELLANEOUS ***STOCKS*** IN NEW YORK–***1897***.

| STOCKS | January. | February. | March. | April. | May. | June. |
|---|---|---|---|---|---|---|
| | Low. High. | Low. High. | Low. High. | Low. High. | Low. High. | Low. High. |
| Chic. Burl. & Qu. | 69 3/8 – 77 1/4 | 73 1/4 – 75 7/8 | 69 5/8 – 78 1/2 | 69 1/2 – 73 5/8 | 72 – 77 | 77 1/4 – 85 |
| Chic. Mil. & St. P. | 72 3/4 – 77 3/8 | 74 1/8 – 77 1/8 | 71 1/4 – 78 1/2 | 69 1/4 – 73 7/8 | 71 3/4 – 76 | 76 1/8 – 83 1/4 |
| Chic. & No'west. | 102 1/4 – 105 3/4 | 103 – 105 5/8 | 103 1/8 – 110 3/4 | 101 3/4 – 105 1/4 | 102 3/4 – 107 3/8 | 107 1/2 – 118 1/4 |
| Chic. R. I. & Pa. | 65 7/8 – 70 | 65 3/8 – 69 | 60 5/8 – 69 5/8 | 60 1/4 – 63 1/2 | 61 1/2 – 66 3/8 | 66 1/4 – 76 3/8 |
| Louisv. & Nash. | 47 5/8 – 52 1/2 | 48 5/8 – 51 7/8 | 44 1/2 – 50 5/8 | 40 1/8 – 46 7/8 | 43 – 46 1/4 | 46 1/8 – 52 1/8 |
| Missouri Pacific | 20 – 24 1/4 | 19 1/4 – 23 | 14 1/2 – 22 3/4 | 13 3/4 – 16 1/8 | 10 – 15 1/4 | 14 3/4 – 20 1/2 |
| No. Pacific Ry. vot. tr. rec. | 13 – 15 5/8 | 13 7/8 – 16 3/8 | 11 1/4 – 14 3/4 | 11 – 13 1/4 | 12 – 13 3/8 | 13 – 15 3/8 |
| Pref. v. tr. rec. | 32 1/8 – 38 1/8 | 36 1/8 – 38 7/8 | 33 1/2 – 38 1/8 | 33 1/8 – 37 | 34 – 38 3/8 | 38 1/8 – 43 5/8 |
| Union Pacific | 6 1/4 – 10 | 6 1/2 – 7 5/8 | 5 1/2 – 7 3/8 | 4 1/2 – 6 1/8 | 5 3/8 – 7 5/8 | 5 5/8 – 8 |
| Am. Sugar R. Co | 110 – 118 3/4 | 110 1/8 – 117 5/8 | 109 1/8 – 118 3/8 | 109 3/4 – 115 | 112 1/8 – 118 | 115 – 130 |
| Am. Tobacco Co. | 73 1/4 – 79 1/2 | 67 1/2 – 75 5/8 | 71 1/8 – 79 3/8 | 68 1/2 – 75 1/8 | 67 3/4 – 72 3/4 | 71 1/8 – 79 3/4 |
| Chicago Gas Co. | 73 1/4 – 79 1/8 | 75 3/8 – 78 3/4 | 75 3/4 – 81 5/8 | 77 5/8 – 84 3/8 | 78 3/4 – 84 | 83 1/2 – 96 5/8 |
| Peoples' G.-L. & C., Ch. | ...... – ...... | ...... – ...... | ...... – ...... | ...... – ...... | ...... – ...... | ...... – ...... |
| West. Union Tel. | 82 3/4 – 86 | 81 – 84 1/2 | 82 1/4 – 86 1/2 | 77 1/4 – 82 1/2 | 75 3/8 – 80 3/8 | 78 3/4 – 85 |

* All assessments paid. † 1st instalment paid.

‡ 2nd instalment paid.

| STOCKS | July. | August. | September. | October. | November. | December. |
|---|---|---|---|---|---|---|
| | Low. High. | Low. High. | Low. High. | Low. High. | Low. High. | Low. High. |
| Chic. Burl. & Qu. | 81 3/4 – 89 3/4 | 87 1/2 – 99 1/4 | 96 3/8 – 102 1/4 | 91 7/8 – 99 1/2 | 89 3/4 – 96 3/4 | 94 5/8 – 100 7/8 |
| Chic. Mil. & St. P. | 81 3/4 – 89 | 86 7/8 – 96 | 94 3/8 – 102 | 91 7/8 – 98 3/8 | 89 – 93 7/8 | 92 3/4 – 96 3/4 |
| Chic. & No'west. | 115 3/8 – 118 1/2 | 117 3/8 – 121 3/4 | 120 1/2 – 132 1/2 | 121 3/8 – 127 7/8 | 117 – 123 3/4 | 119 3/4 – 124 1/8 |
| Chic. R. I. & Pa. | 73 – 83 1/8 | 81 5/8 – 91 3/8 | 89 3/8 – 97 1/4 | 84 7/8 – 92 1/8 | 81 1/8 – 88 1/2 | 88 3/8 – 92 1/8 |
| Louisv. & Nash. | 49 1/4 – 55 5/8 | 55 3/8 – 62 3/8 | 57 5/8 – 63 7/8 | 54 3/8 – 61 1/4 | 51 3/8 – 56 3/4 | 54 5/8 – 58 5/8 |
| Missouri Pacific | 18 5/8 – 27 | 24 3/4 – 39 1/4 | 32 1/8 – 40 1/4 | 27 1/2 – 35 1/4 | 25 7/8 – 31 5/8 | 29 1/2 – 35 7/8 |
| No. Pacific Ry. vot. tr. rec. | 13 5/8 – 15 5/8 | 15 1/4 – 18 5/8 | 17 3/4 – 21 7/8 | 17 1/2 – 21 1/8 | 16 1/2 – 19 1/2 | 19 1/8 – 22 3/8 |
| Pref. v. tr. rec. | 39 7/8 – 45 1/2 | 45 5/8 – 51 5/8 | 49 7/8 – 57 | 50 1/2 – 55 7/8 | 48 5/8 – 56 1/4 | 55 5/8 – 61 5/8 |
| Union Pacific | 5 7/8 – 8 1/4 | 7 3/4 – †18 1/4 | †16 3/4 – †24 7/8 | †20 1/4 – ‡27 3/4 | ‡18 3/4 – *24 1/8 | *23 7/8 – *26 1/2 |
| Am. Sugar R. Co | 125 5/8 – 146 1/4 | 138 1/2 – 157 3/8 | 142 3/4 – 159 1/2 | 137 – 150 1/4 | 126 3/4 – 143 | 135 3/8 – 145 1/2 |
| Am. Tobacco Co. | 73 1/2 – 85 | 83 – 96 3/4 | 87 – 96 1/8 | 78 7/8 – 90 1/4 | 78 1/4 – 83 | 81 1/2 – 90 1/8 |
| Chicago Gas Co. | 92 3/8 – 99 5/8 | 99 3/8 – 103 3/4 | 98 1/8 – 108 3/4 | 87 1/8 – 102 | 92 1/2 – 97 3/8 | ...... – ...... |
| Peoples' G.-L. & C., Ch. | ...... – ...... | ...... – ...... | ...... – ...... | 92 1/2 – 94 5/8 | 91 – 96 3/4 | 93 3/4 – 97 5/8 |
| West. Union Tel. | 83 1/2 – 86 1/2 | 85 7/8 – 94 1/2 | 89 – 96 3/4 | 87 1/8 – 91 7/8 | 84 1/2 – 88 1/2 | 87 1/2 – 91 7/8 |

* All assessments paid. † 1st instalment paid.

‡ 2nd instalment paid.

## YEARLY RANGE IN PRICES OF ACTIVE STOCKS.

The extreme fluctuations in the prices of active stocks for four years past are shown in the table presented below. It will be noticed that not only do we give the highest and lowest prices in each year, but the month and day when such prices were made.

| STOCKS | Year 1894. | | Year 1895. | |
|---|---|---|---|---|
| | Lowest. | Highest. | Lowest. | Highest. |
| RAILROADS | | | | |
| Chic. Burl & Quincy | 68 5/8 Dec. 1 | 84 1/8 Mar. 21 | 69 Mar. 4 | 92 5/8 July 29 |
| Chic. Mil. & St. Paul | 54 1/4 Jan. 3 | 67 3/8 Sept. 6 | 53 7/8 Mar. 9 | 78 7/8 Sept. 4 |
| Chic & Northwestern | 96 1/4 Dec. 5 | 110 3/8 June 7 | 87 3/8 Mar. 4 | 107 1/2 Feb. 16 |
| Chic. R. I. & Pacific | 58 1/2 Oct. 11 | 72 3/8 Apr. 7 | 59 Dec. 21 | 84 3/8 Aug. 28 |
| Louisville & Nash | 40 7/8 Jan. 12 | 57 3/8 Sept. 22 | 39 Dec. 20 | 66 1/8 Sept. 4 |
| Missouri Pacific | 18 1/8 Jan. 5 | 32 1/2 Apr. 7 | 18 5/8 Mar. 11 | 42 1/2 Sept. 9 |
| No. Pa. vot. tr. ctfs. | .............. | .............. | .............. | .............. |
| Union Pacific | 7 July 30 | 22 1/2 Mar. 31 | 4 Dec. 30 | 17 1/2 May 11 |
| MISCELLANEOUS | | | | |
| Amer. Sugar Ref. Co. | 75 5/8 Feb. 1 | 114 7/8 Aug. 21 | 86 1/2 Jan. 3 | 121 3/8 June 13 |
| Amer. Tobacco Co. | 69 7/8 Jan. 2 | 107 Aug. 27 | 63 Dec. 9 | 117 May 27 |
| Chicago Gas | 58 3/4 Jan. 3 | 80 June 35 | 49 7/8 July 16 | 78 1/4 Jan. 11 |
| General Electric | 30 3/8 Jan. 3 | 45 1/8 Mar. 8 | 20 Dec. 20 | 41 Sept. 9 |
| People's Gas L. & Coke (Chic.) | .............. | .............. | .............. | .............. |
| Western Union Tel. | 80 7/8 Jan. 3 | 92 1/2 Sept. 11 | 82 1/2 Dec. 20 | 95 3/8 Sept. 3 |

| STOCKS | Year 1896. | | | | Year 1897. | | | |
|---|---|---|---|---|---|---|---|---|
| | Lowest. | | Highest. | | Lowest. | | Highest. | |
| RAILROADS | | | | | | | | |
| Chic. Burl & Quincy | 53 | Aug. 7 | 85 3/4 | Nov. 10 | 69 3/8 | Jan. 5 | 102 1/4 | Sept. 20 |
| Chic. Mil. & St. Paul | 59 7/8 | Aug. 10 | 80 | Nov. 4 | 69 1/4 | Apr. 19 | 102 | Sept. 15 |
| Chic & Northwestern | 85 1/8 | Aug. 10 | 106 3/4 | Apr. 23 | 101 3/4 | Apr. 19 | 132 1/2 | Sept. 15 |
| Chic. R. I. & Pacific | 49 1/4 | Aug. 7 | 74 7/8 | Feb. 24 | 60 1/4 | Apr. 19 | 97 1/4 | Sept. 20 |
| Louisville & Nash | 37 1/8 | Aug. 26 | 55 3/8 | Feb. 24 | 40 1/8 | Apr. 19 | 63 7/8 | Sept. 3 |
| Missouri Pacific | 15 | Aug. 7 | 29 3/4 | Apr. 24 | 10 | May 6 | 40 1/4 | Sept. 7 |
| No. Pa. vot. tr. ctfs. | 12 1/4 | Dec. 19 | 14 3/8 | Dec. 30 | 11 | Apr. 19 | 22 3/4 | Dec. 15 |
| Union Pacific | 3 1/2 | Jan. 7 | 12 1/2 | Nov. 4 | 4 1/2 | Apr. 19 | ‡27 3/4 | Oct. 20 |
| MISCELLANEOUS | | | | | | | | |
| Amer. Sugar Ref. Co. | 95 | Aug. 10 | 126 5/8 | Apr. 21 | 109 1/8 | Mar. 29 | 159 1/2 | Sept. 3 |
| Amer. Tobacco Co. | 51 | Aug. 10 | 95 | Apr. 2 | 67 1/2 | Feb. 15 | 96 3/8 | Aug. 9 |
| Chicago Gas | 44 3/8 | Aug. 8 | 78 3/4 | Nov. 7 | 73 1/4 | Jan. 5 | 108 3/4 | Sept. 18 |
| General Electric | 20 | July 16 | 39 1/2 | Mar. 13 | 28 3/8 | May 17 | 41 3/4 | Sept. 15 |
| People's Gas L. & Coke (Chic.) | . . . . . . . . . . . . . . | | . . . . . . . . . . . . . . | | 91 | Nov. 26 | 96 3/4 | Nov. 10 |
| Western Union Tel. | 72 3/4 | Aug. 10 | 90 1/4 | Nov. 11 | 75 3/8 | May 7 | 96 3/4 | Sept. 11 |

‡ All instalments paid

# CAMPAIGN DIAGRAM

Diagram Illustrating in a general way the yearly
Grand Campaigns in Sugar Stock from 1894 to
1898. There are small campaigns "skirmishes"
in addition that do not show here.

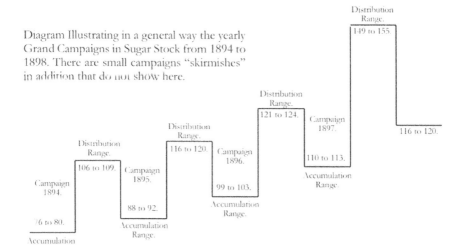

# STOCK CHARTS

## BURLINGTON

**BURLINGTON**

ACCUMULATION

1897
JANUARY | FEBRUARY | MARCH | APRIL | MAY | JUNE

X Feb. 27

DISTRIBUTION

X Aug. 20

X Nov. 19

1897
JULY | AUGUST | SEPTEMBER | OCTOBER | NOVEMBER | DECEMBER

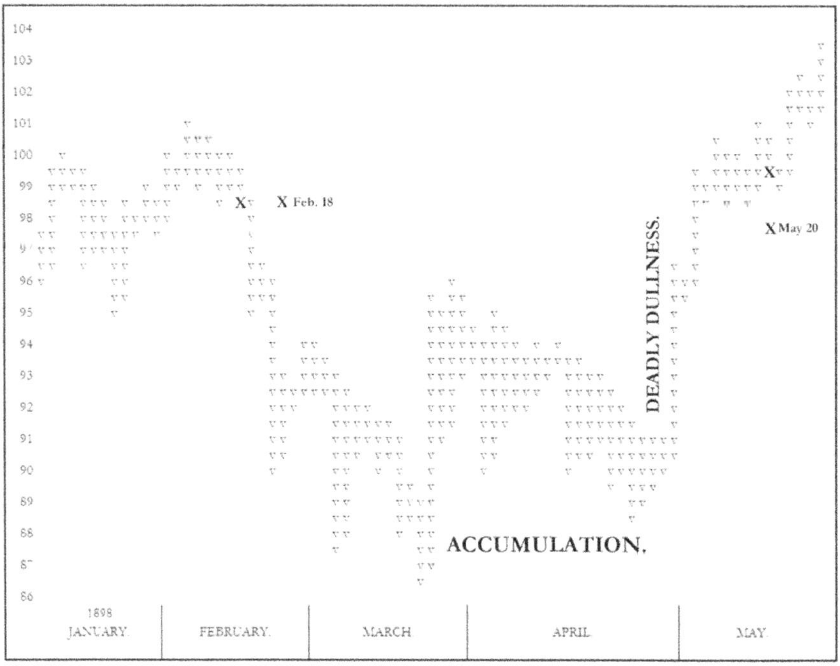
104
103
102
101
100
99
98
97
96
95
94
93
92
91
90
89
88
87
86
X Feb. 18
X May 20
DEADLY DULLNESS.
ACCUMULATION.
1898
JANUARY.
FEBRUARY.
MARCH
APRIL
MAY.

# ST PAUL

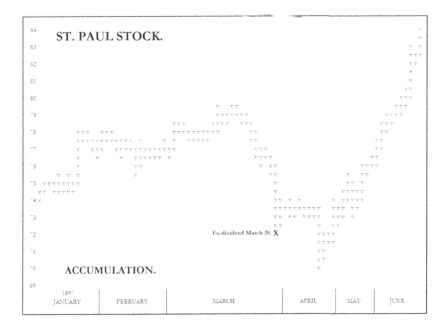

DISTRIBUTION.
Ex-dividend Sept. 28.
Small Bull Campaign.
JULY
AUGUST
SEPTEMBER
OCTOBER
NOVEMBER
DECEMBER

ACCUMULATION.
Rapid and wide fluctuation due to
"War Scare."

# SUGAR

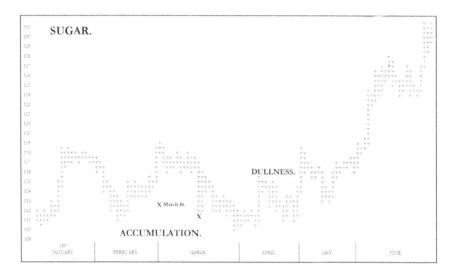

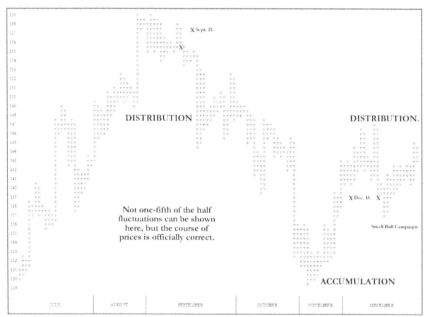

"REMEMBER THE MAINE,"

X Ex-dividend March 15.

X

ACCUMULATION.

The wide and rapid fluctuations
here due to the "War Scare."

| 1898 JANUARY | FEBRUARY | MARCH. | APRIL | MAY |

# SUGAR TRAPS

| DISTRIBUTION. | June 20 to June 28, 1895. |
|---|---|

Sugar Trap No. 1.

| DISTRIBUTION. | | | June 20 to June 28, 1896. |
|---|---|---|---|
| 125 ᴠ ᴠ | | ᴠ | ᴠ |
| ᴠ ᴠ ᴠ ᴠ | | ᴠ ᴠ | ᴠ ᴠ |
| 124 ᴠ ᴠ ᴠ ᴠ ᴠ | ᴠ | ᴠ ᴠ ᴠ | ᴠ ᴠ ᴠ |
| ᴠ | ᴠ ᴠ ᴠ ᴠ ᴠ | ᴠ ᴠ ᴠ ᴠ ᴠ ᴠ ᴠ ᴠ ᴠ | ᴠ |
| 123 | ᴠ ᴠ ᴠ ᴠ ᴠ | ᴠ ᴠ ᴠ ᴠ ᴠ ᴠ ᴠ ᴠ ᴠ ᴠ ᴠ | ᴠ |
| ᴠ ᴠ ᴠ | ᴠ | ᴠ ᴠ ᴠ ᴠ ᴠ ᴠ ᴠ ᴠ ᴠ | ᴠ ᴠ ᴠ ᴠ ᴠ |
| 122 | ᴠ | ᴠ ᴠ ᴠ ᴠ ᴠ ᴠ ᴠ ᴠ ᴠ | ᴠ ᴠ ᴠ ᴠ ᴠ |
| | ᴠ ᴠ ᴠ | ᴠ ᴠ ᴠ | ᴠ ᴠ ᴠ ᴠ |
| 121 | ᴠ ᴠ | ᴠ ᴠ ᴠ ᴠ | ᴠ |
| | ᴠ ᴠ | ᴠ ᴠ ᴠ | ᴠ |
| 120 | ᴠ | ᴠ | ᴠ |
| 119 | | | ᴠ |
| | | | ᴠ |
| 118 | | | ᴠ |
| | | | ᴠ |
| 117 | **Sugar Trap No. 2.** | | ᴠ |
| | | | ᴠ |
| 116 | | | ᴠ |
| | | | ᴠ ᴠ |
| 115 | | | ᴠ ᴠ ᴠ |
| | | | ᴠ ᴠ ᴠ |
| 114 | | | ᴠ ᴠ ᴠ |
| | | | ᴠ ᴠ ᴠ |
| 113 | | | ᴠ ᴠ ᴠ |
| | | | ᴠ ᴠ |
| 112 | | | ᴠ |
| | | | ᴠ ᴠ |
| 111 | | | ᴠ ᴠ ᴠ |
| | | | ᴠ ᴠ ᴠ |
| 110 | | | ᴠ ᴠ ᴠ |
| | | | ᴠ ᴠ ᴠ |
| 109 | | | ᴠ ᴠ ᴠ |
| | | | ᴠ ᴠ |
| 108 | | | ᴠ ᴠ |

# THE END.

# ABOUT THE ORIGINAL EDITION

*The Game in Wall Street* was originally published in 1898 by J S Ogilvie Publishing Company, 57 Rose Street, New York City. Founded in 1878, the company mainly specialized in 'railroad literature' – paperbacks sold on trains. The company's output consisted of adventure stories, humor titles, song books, recitations, volumes of advice on courtship, and other self-help titles.

The credited author of *The Game in Wall Street* was "Hoyle", the quote marks suggesting the name is a pseudonym, although elsewhere the author has been listed as William E. Forrest Hoyle, about whom nothing further is known.

This new edition of the text includes a preface and conclusion by market guru Clem Chambers.

# ABOUT CLEM CHAMBERS

Clem Chambers is CEO of ADVFN, Europe and South America's leading financial website.

A broadcast and print media regular, Clem Chambers is a familiar face and frequent co-presenter on **CNBC** and **CNBC Europe.** He is a seasoned guest and market commentator on **BBC News, Fox News, CNBC Arabia Newsnight, Al Jazeera, CNN, SKY News, TF1,** Canada's **Business News Network** and numerous US radio stations.

He is renowned for calling the markets and predicted the end of the bull market back in January 2007 and the following crash. He has appeared on ITV's **News at Ten** and **Evening News** discussing failures in the banking system and featured prominently in the **Money Programme's** *Credit Crash Britain: HBOS — Breaking the Bank* and on the BBC's *City Uncovered: When Markets Go Mad.*

Clem has written investment columns for **Wired Magazine**, which described him as a 'Market Maven', **The Daily Mail, The Daily Telegraph** and **The Daily Express** and currently writes for **Forbes, Business Mirror, Index Trader, Traders** and **YourTradingEdge**.

He was The Alchemist – stock tipster – in **The Business** for over three years and has been published in titles including: **CityAM, Investors Chronicle, Traders Magazine, Stocks and Commodities**, the **Channel 4** website, **SFO** and **Accountancy Age** and has been quoted in many more publications including all of the main UK national newspapers. He also wrote a monthly spread betting column in gambling magazine **Inside Edge**.

Clem has written several books for ADVFN Books, including **101 Ways To Pick Stock Market Winners, A Beginner's Guide to Value Investing, The Death of Wealth** and **Letters to my Broker**.

In the last few years he has become a successful financial thriller writer, authoring **The Twain Maxim, The Armageddon Trade, Kusanagi** and **The First Horseman**.

Clem also writes for the ADVFN newspaper and has a premium newsletter for subscribers, the **Diary of a Contrarian Investor** (http://www.advfn.com/newsletter/clemchambers/).

# ANOTHER CLASSIC TEXT FROM ADVFN BOOKS

## LETTERS TO MY BROKER

### P.S. What do you think of the Market?

*"Why is it the minute I sell my stocks, no matter which they are, right away they go up?"*

Meet Joe, a rich but hapless investor who makes every mistake possible. Just when you think he's learnt something, he finds a new way to lose money.

Populated by rogues, hucksters and fools *Letters to my Broker* is the classic comedy of errors revived for a new generation that teaches you the rules to trading the stock market haven't changed in the 94 years since its original publication.

*"I want some advice. Not that I'll follow it."*

Aided by the acerbic commentary of No. 1 bestselling author and ADVFN CEO Clem Chambers, *Letters to my Broker* tells you where Joe's going wrong, what you should do to keep your shirt and how to avoid his hilarious errors.

Stock market tips so old they're new: Read *Letters to my Broker* and trade like it's 1919.

Available in paperback and for the Kindle.